BLEEDING SPIRITS

A COMBAT SOLDIER'S MEMOIR
OF THE VIETNAM WAR
1968–1969

Former Infantry Sgt. Robert E. Jewell

Sweetgrass Books

HELENA, MONTANA

Published by Tom Gannon, 2020

ISBN 978-1-59152-264-5

Edited by Marisa Diaz-Waian with the help of Robert E. Jewell's daughters, Sheri Erhardt and Holly Jewell, and friend, Tom Gannon.

Cover photo of Robert E. Jewell. All other photographs courtesy of Robert E. Jewell's collection unless credited otherwise.

Title page photo, left to right: Frank Guffey, Robert Jewell, and Louis Givens.

For more information or to order extra copies of this book call Farcountry Press toll free at (800) 821-3874.

sweetgrassbooks
an imprint of Farcountry Press

Produced by Sweetgrass Books
PO Box 5630, Helena, MT 59604; (800) 821-3874;
www.sweetgrassbooks.com.

Produced and printed in the United States of America.

23   22   21   20   1   2   3   4   5

To my family, friends, and fellow soldiers.

To the innocent civilians and scarred countryside(s).

To the peaceful protestors and conscientious objectors.

And to all those affected by the harsh realities of war.

A Caution Before Reading

BECAUSE I INTENDED for even my grandchildren to be able to read this book, I have tried to tell all stories with a minimum amount of graphic details and harsh language. However, I also needed to say enough about the events so that the brutality of combat and emotions involved are adequately represented. Forgive me, but sometimes in war, "golly gee whiz" just doesn't cut it! As such, while I have tried to use the bare minimum to make my point, readers will encounter some "F-bombs" and a few mentions of physical destruction.

Friends who have already read *Bleeding Spirits* recommend that individuals under the age of eighteen should not read some of the chapters. The ADULT ONLY chapters include "Firefight In An Artillery Barrage" and "War Crimes."

Other chapters may be less violent and frightening but can still be upsetting. Therefore, please read this book with the mindset that the content of *Bleeding Spirits* is NOT about bad things that happened to me…but rather about my surviving these things and thriving! Truly, I have had a very good life since Vietnam. And, in some important ways, I am *better* for having experienced that war. I believe that the events of life, on any scale, are our teachers.

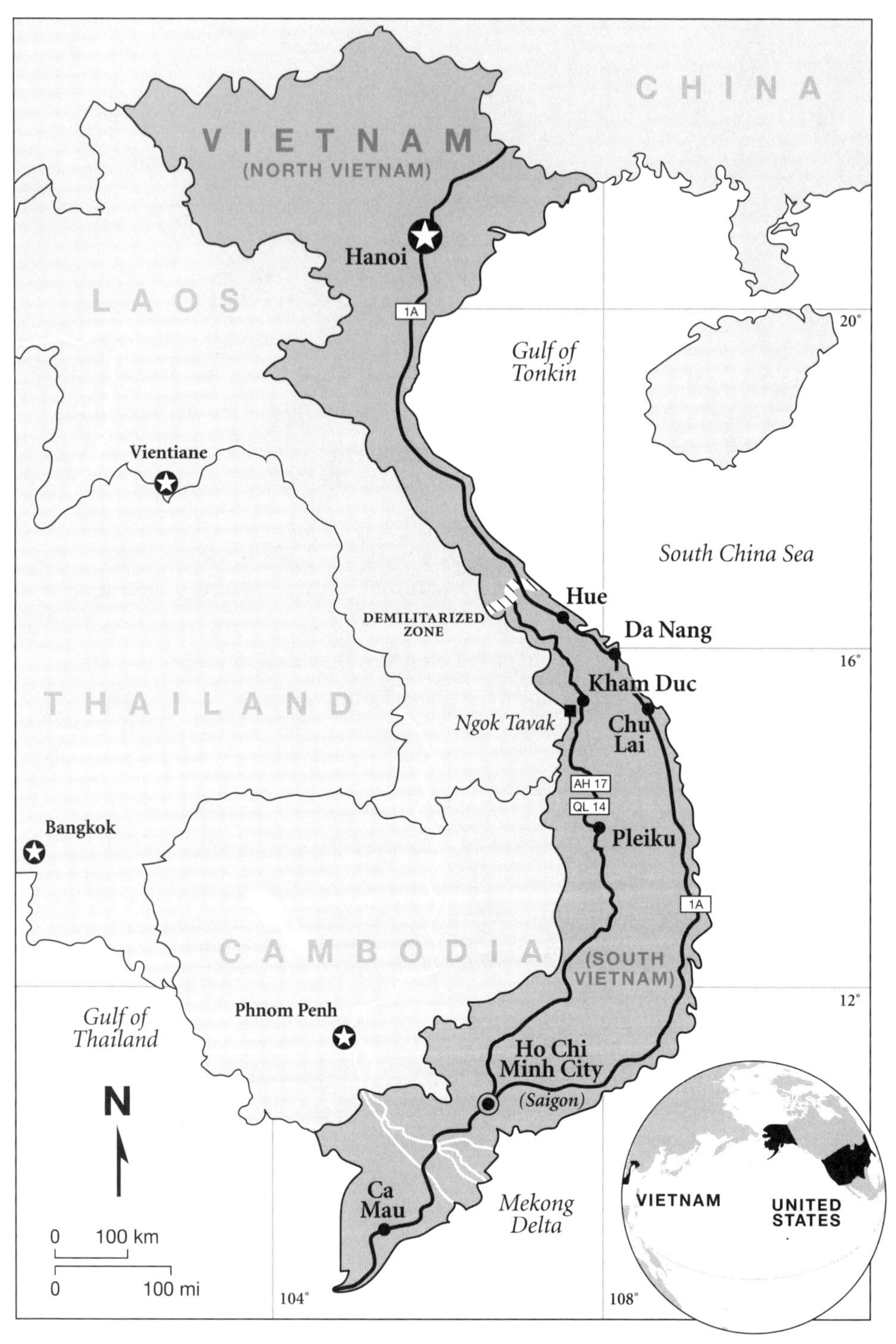

Vietnam and Southeast Asia

Introduction

Bleeding Spirits consists of a series of memories from my time in Vietnam. I wrote these memories for:

Myself—To get the memories out of my head and onto paper. (This process resulted in a noticeable lightening of a mental burden when finished!)

Others—For those who want an insightful look into some of the untold workings of war and its warriors.

My Family and Friends—So that they can better understand why I am "a bit quirky" at times.

To the best of my ability, I have attempted to present these memories to you chronologically. However, as is the nature of memory, war, and life after war, the walls of time can often disappear. What is more, I truly believe that few memories ever stand alone in isolation. Instead, they become the building blocks of who we are. And to separate them *completely* from one another—like untangled specimen in petri dishes—is both unrealistic and unfair. That said, I do my best to unravel them beneath time's scope with as much accuracy as possible.

CONTENTS

Preface

I CHOSE THE TITLE *BLEEDING SPIRITS* while reflecting on how my spirit still felt sharp pain while writing some of my combat memories several decades after my physical combat wounds had healed.

My spirit does not bleed for just myself. It also bleeds for all of the war troops on both sides. Had our countries not been at war, we troops might instead have met as friendly visitors, as we do today.

My spirit also bleeds when I think of the millions of civilians involved! Some of these were Vietnamese civilians who got caught in the deadly crossfires of war in their homeland. And some of these were American civilians, allied families, and friends who—thousands of miles away—suffered greatly when their loved ones returned with horrible psychological scars, maimed, or in a pine box.

Then there were the civilian peace protestors and conscientious objectors whose hearts firmly believed that the Vietnam War was a tragic mistake. Among other things, those people were brutally beaten by policemen whose own hearts firmly believed that the protestors were cowardly and un-American. In the end, the protesters likely shortened the war and saved lives! In the end, many of those policemen later regretted what they did to those young men and women who were other people's sons and daughters.

Grief, hate, guilt, injustice, prejudice, and shame all slice the human spirit. Our spirits bleed.

Robert Jewell's graduating class at Fort Lewis Washington, 1967.
Robert is in the third row from top, fourth from the left.

MY ENTERING THE WAR: THE EFFECT ON MY FAMILY

I HAD BEEN WORKING on a highway construction crew in Glacier Park in the summer of 1967. I had the "perfect job!"—high wages, working outdoors surrounded by breathtaking scenery with four of my high school buddies and an abundance of college-aged girls who worked at the East Glacier Inn near where I was housed. Life couldn't have been sweeter. I felt like I was living and working in heaven!

One sunny day in July, our mail arrived, forwarded as usual by our parents back in Great Falls. On that day, however, one of my letters was a thick envelope with my Dad's handwritten note written across it, "We hope this isn't what we think it is." In the upper left corner I read the sender… "Department of the Army of the Unites States." I felt a hollow feeling in the pit of my stomach. I opened it, and with my friends anxiously looking over my shoulder, I read the first words: "Greetings: You are hereby ordered for induction into the Armed Forces of the United States." F**k, I'd been drafted. The beautiful sunny Glacier Park afternoon instantly turned dark and cloudy over me. I had suddenly just been ordered to a new job—perhaps in hell!

The Vietnam War had already become increasingly unpopular and was viewed with suspicion by many people. One of our best friends, Joe Klemencic, had been killed in Vietnam just months earlier! Some of my angry friends were advising me to pack up and move to Canada.

Back home with my family the following weekend, I discussed my situation with my dad who was a Marine in World War II. My dad was always a cool-headed guy, and I deeply respected his integrity and what he said. We discussed my options: (1) Go into the military to serve my two years; (2) Reject my draft order and be sent to federal prison for up to 20 years, or; (3) Flee to Canada—but face immediate arrest and prison if I came back home.

None of those choices seemed very good. Noting a positive consideration for the military option, Dad pointed out the attractive veterans' benefits of receiving the GI Bill's college education and Federal Job Preference. Despite the advantages in this option, however, I could tell that he was also fearful about losing a son. The consequence of refusing induction was to live as either a fugitive or as a criminal/ex-con. That idea felt repugnant! So, I chose to become a soldier in the United States Army. I prayed hard that God would bring me back home alive and whole.

About four months later, having completed both basic and infantry training, I returned home in uniform for a month's leave prior to my being shipped out to Vietnam. My family and friends were surprised at how much muscle I had gained. Everyone was glad to see me, but we were all aware that this could be the last time that I would be home alive. This fear was reinforced nightly by the *Huntley-Brinkley Report,* a popular NBC News program that always showed graphic footage of Vietnam War combat. My family and I watched the war footage with silent intensity. None of us enjoyed watching those battle scenes under my circumstances, but morbid curiosity drew us to the TV's battle scenes like moths to a flame. Many a prayer went through our minds as we watched dead or wounded soldiers being taken off the field of battle. And we all were painfully aware that in a matter of days I would be one of those soldiers in the war zone. The concept seemed totally surreal to me!

At the end of my month leave, I shipped out to Vietnam. My mom and dad would continue to watch the *Huntley-Brinkley Report* every night—but from then on, they would closely look to see the faces of the wounded and dead soldiers…terrified that one of the faces would be mine. My mother would tell me later that they were tortured night and day by that horrible fear.

A few months into my tour of Vietnam, a cruel incident unfolded for my parents. My mom and dad looked out their living room window one cold gray day and saw—to their absolute horror—two uniformed Army officers in a green government sedan parked in front of our home at 2115 7th Ave. North. The soldiers were looking up at the address on our house! My parents' poor hearts sank! My mother had seen this same scene in her neighborhood all too often during World War II. It always meant one thing: the dreaded message, *"On behalf of the United States Army, we deeply regret to inform you of the death of your...."* My parents' spirits started to bleed heavily.

After an agonizing minute, the two officers finally got out of their car and started up the walkway to our door. My mother later told me that they burst into tears of terrible grief, held each other tight, and cringed behind the front door. It seemed clear that the dreaded moment had arrived! The soldiers finally knocked. My father painfully opened the door.

The soldiers immediately saw the anguish on my parents' faces. Taken aback, the soldiers spoke with a very apologetic tone. "We're very sorry to be interrupting you, sir," one of them began, "but can you please tell us where 2112½ 7th Avenue North is?"

The two officers were just looking for a recruit who rented the small house behind the house across the street! My parents told me that their minds went through every possible human emotion. In an instant they were jerked from "the certainty of their son's death" to an incredibly badly-timed circumstance. My dad's anguish and shock burst from his chest in an angry outrage: "We have a son fighting in Vietnam!" he yelled through his tears at the two hapless soldiers. "You nearly scared us to death! Get off my porch. You're looking for someone behind that house across the street!"

Slamming the door closed, my parents clutched each other again—this time crying huge tears of relief—victims of a horribly cruel set of circumstances. By the grace of God, no other soldiers came to our house after that. Still, my parents suffered great torment during my long 416 days of combat. When I finally walked off the jet on March 29, 1969, safely home at last, I was shocked to see how my mom and dad had aged during that time. Although I had been wounded three times and suffered tremendous misery, I think that my parents suffered even more! There is no greater pain than the death of one's child, and Mom and Dad lived that possibility every day that I was in Vietnam. My heart feels heavy every time I think about their long torment. May God have a special comfort for them in heaven.

Nearly 30 years later, at one of our annual Jewell family reunions, some of us were sitting in my breakfast nook conversing about the early days. I brought up the fact that none of us had ever talked about my being in Vietnam...what it was like for me or what it was like for them! *Nothing* ever said...no questions about it ever! I expressed that it seemed very strange that something so important was never discussed.

I hadn't thought about what their response might be, but what happened next totally surprised me. My sweet little 88-year-old mother lowered her head and began to weep—nearly thirty years after my time in Vietnam! After a few seconds, she spoke words that wrenched my heart. "You know, all the time that you were over there," she said, "your Dad and I prayed day and night that you would be able to survive and come home again. But we weren't prepared for how you would be if you returned." And then she added, "*The son that we saw off to war...never came back.*"

I was stunned by her words and deeply saddened. With tears in my eyes, I blurted, "Mommm! Mom, I tried so *hard* to show you all that I was okay!" She replied, "I know, but the look in your eyes showed that you weren't the same boy at all. It was too hard to talk about."

I can't remember how the conversation continued, but I remember feeling so shitty that—after all of their agonizing while I was in Vietnam—their heartache continued even after I came home alive and un-crippled. I realized, only then, that I wasn't the great actor that I had always thought I'd been. Despite my most sincere and determined motivation, I was an amateur. I still feel cutting sorrow for what my parents went through because of my going to Vietnam.

Toward the end of my stint as an infantryman, a platoonmate told me that he had simply lied to his parents about what he was doing in Vietnam; he told them that he worked in the safety of a base camp laundry. A simple lie, I thought...a brilliant lie! Immediately I wished that I had thought of that idea from the start! Despite what I had learned in my Catholic upbringing, some lies are actually good and humane!

Upon hearing my platoonmate's clever lie, I quickly wrote a letter home telling everyone that I had been transferred to the brigade's base camp laundry! Though still in the infantry, and getting wounded another time, at least my family would get some respite from the fear that their son would die in combat. At least I *hoped* that would be the case.

Now, however, as I write about "my humane lie," I'm not so sure that it actually ended up helping my family for long! I just now remembered that I had *written my lie* to my family—but not to my friends! I had never felt a need to lie to my friends because I didn't think that my friends would worry so deeply.

The problem with my not telling my friends the same lie as my parents is that some of my friends often visited my mom and dad while I was in Vietnam...and it is probable that my parents would have told them how relieved they were that I was "safely doing laundry now." If that likely conversation happened, I would suppose that my friends then expressed surprise that I had never told them, which would then have raised some doubts in my parents' minds that I was really out of combat. After all, "Why wouldn't their son have not also told his friends about his safe new job?!"

Did my lie fail? I'll never know because my family never discussed my war life upon my return, and now my parents are no longer alive for me to ask. Damn, I'm still worrying about my parents' pain—and they're no longer even alive! Man, does war ever suck...STILL!

WELCOME TO VIETNAM,
YOU POOR BASTARDS!

I WAS ONE OF A PLANE-FULL of new replacement troops that were flying from Fort Lewis, Washington to Chu Lai Air Base, Vietnam in January 1968. As if knowing that I was heading into combat wasn't bad enough, I was extremely ill from a severe case of pneumonia and a horrible ear infection…and our transportation was a damn *cargo* jet! That meant poor pressurization and having to sit on *cargo straps* instead of passenger seats for a marathon seventeen-hour flight!

Sitting on those cargo straps and bars for so long would have been my worst misery had it not been for the excruciating pain that I felt in my ears! It felt like my eardrums would explode any second. Oh yes… and there was no getting out of your seat for the entire flight except for when it was finally your turn to use the plane's one toilet. I didn't know it at the time, but this miserable *flight from hell* was a relatively sweet experience compared to the months with my soon-to-be combat family, the *company from hell!*

After an incredibly miserable flight, we were all actually relieved to touch down in Vietnam's combat zone. Once the jet had finally rolled to a stop on the huge Chu Lai military airfield, we were ordered to rise, put on our combat packs, and disembark. Typical of a cargo jet, its huge door spanned the whole rear of the airplane. It lowered to form a wide ramp down to the airstrip. I'll never forget the shock when that big door opened! Blinding sunlight blasted in along with air that was so hot and humid that our lungs immediately seized shut! With a half mile of black-top in every direction, the air temperature was over 140 degrees!

Immediately, a sergeant charged to the top of the ramp and bellowed in a hostile roar, "Get off my airplane! Get off! Get off! Now! Now! Now!!!" The new soldiers who were nearest the door scrambled off first with the sergeant *swinging a stick at them* as they flew past! Chased off the plane like a bunch of dogs, we were all ordered to line up "at attention" in platoon formations as several other antagonistic sergeants joined in on the screaming. None of us had been expecting a nice vacation in Vietnam—but shit-oh-dear! This reception party was the rudest party we'd ever been invited to!

Soon we were herded aboard uncovered side-railed army "cattle trucks." While waiting, packed like sardines, an army jeep with two extremely tanned GI's drove up beside us and hollered cordially, "Welcome to Vietnam, boys! What unit are you assigned to?" We answered, "Charlie Company, 2/1 of the 196th Light Infantry Brigade."

The two smiling GI's faces turned visibly solemn. "Aw shit!" they both answered back with tight voices. Their response was the very last thing we wanted to hear!

Several of us responded in nervous unison, "What do you mean?" The driver slowly shook his head and replied, "Charlie 2/1 is always in bad shit! In fact, they nearly got wiped out just two or three weeks ago... you guys are the replacements." I'm certain that there wasn't a single one of us aboard that cattle truck who didn't suddenly feel ugly black clouds gathering over our heads. "Clearly, Toto, we weren't in Kansas anymore."

Soon after arriving, our Chu Lai base came under a huge attack. It was the first week of the Tet Offensive! We new guys hadn't even been issued our weapons yet and we were outraged to be so helpless during the attack. Defenseless, we were herded into large sandbagged Quonset huts where we were assured that only a direct artillery hit would hurt us...which only *slightly* allayed our fears. Suddenly, a *monstrous* explosion bounced us off the ground! I was certain that an atomic bomb had been dropped on the base. "Nothing less than an A-Bomb could create that blast," I thought! The monstrous blast was actually a direct hit on Chu Lai's Ammo Depot. That was where thousands of U.S. bombs, rockets, artillery rounds, etc. were stockpiled. It was estimated to be a seven-kiloton blast! In WWII, the Hiroshima A-Bomb was a nine-kiloton blast!

A few days later, now with our assigned weapons, we were helicoptered out of Chu Lai to join our Charlie Company at Fire Base Ross, about forty miles northwest of Chu Lai's American Division Headquarters. Because of Charlie Company's heavy casualty loss, they were still in "stand down" mode, which means staying back within the relatively safe confines of a protected base without any assigned duties. Normally a company has 100 to 160 soldiers; Charlie Company had been reduced to a mere seventeen bruised and battered survivors of a very horrible battle!

I was assigned to 2nd Platoon, which had four of the seventeen survivors. I was stunned when I met them! One could only talk in a high-pitched rasp because much of his voice box had been shot out. Another had a deep depression in his right upper arm where most of his biceps and triceps had been shot away. A third guy, our medic, had a deep groove running along his jaw line from chin to ear. An enemy bullet had taken a good portion of his flesh and part of his jawbone away, so he had to chew his food on the other side of his mouth. To further our dismay, these survivors told us that this same company had previously lost most of its men in yet another horrible battle several months before this recent one! (The two GI's in the Jeep who had initially greeted us upon our arrival to Vietnam had not exaggerated Charlie Company's plight).

The fourth battered survivor in our 2nd Platoon turned out to be my squad leader, fondly known as "Shorty." ("Shorty" was a childhood nickname; he was actually about six feet tall.) Sandy hair, a deep tan, and a sturdy frame, Shorty strode over to meet us. His tanned shirtless torso was "a quilt" of stitched shrapnel scars.

And despite having been severely battered by combat, he was rarely without a smile. Quietly exuding competence, a deep inner strength, warmth, and charisma, all of the company's other sixteen survivors viewed him with the highest respect. Shorty was "the soldier's soldier." Even officers consulted with him.

We new guys felt a stomach-tightening shock when we met these four battle-toughened veterans who formed the nucleus of our platoon. Seeing their battered but "good enough to return to combat" condition hit us like a ton of bricks with the sickening reality that we had been dropped into a *serious* war zone! I was glad that Shorty would be my squad leader—an encouraging consolation that at least I would be in the best possible hands!

The scarred seventeen survivors portended what we new guys might eventually look like. I had no idea what horrors and tragedies would unfold in the following months, but seeing these survivors on my first day in the field scared me like nothing before in my life.

Then, something drove my fear to even greater depths! At the end of my first day afield, I was eating my C-rations with some other new guys and three of the seventeen survivors. With a weak smile and faux optimism, I attempted some understated humor, "Well, I've only got 360 days left before I'm back home." Rather than chuckles, my joke was met with bitter scorn! "You ain't going home alive," one of the seventeen scolded me. "Ain't none of us going home alive! The best you can hope for is to kill as many gooks as you can before you die...But *none* of us are going home outside of a box!" Others of the seventeen were looking at me "as if I had just declared Santa Claus to be real!" Fellow new recruits, who were with me in our little group, searched faces for "the joke"...but no joke was found in the hardened eyes of the veterans! Then the wide-eyed recruits shot glances at me with looks that seemed to whimper, "Ohhh shit! This is not the horrible war that we watched on TV's *Huntley-Brinkley Report!* ...It's much worse!"

My Charlie Company suffered five more KIA's during my first week, and many more were wounded. Going a whole year in this place without being severely maimed or killed felt like pure childish fantasy! *"Ain't none of us going home alive"* began to feel like proper admonishment.

I felt half-dead already.

THE SOLDIER'S SOLDIER

WITH ONLY SEVENTEEN SURVIVORS remaining from a horrible battle that occurred about two weeks before my arrival, Charlie Company was soon populated mostly by new guys. We called ourselves "replacements." However, combat-hardened guys who had been in Vietnam for a while, usually referred to us new arrivals as FNG's—short for "f**ing new guys." This was obviously not a term of endearment. New guys lacked experience, and having lack of experience was dangerous.

As for myself, my inexperience was compounded by a severe case of pneumonia, which I'd had since infantry training six weeks earlier. Not only could I not speak without going into a long coughing fit, I was also severely weakened and half deaf from a horrible infection in both ears. This lasted for my first two or three weeks in 'Nam before I finally healed. While I was still sick, however, it was extra terrifying for me because I was always afraid that I would miss a critical instruction. For Battalion Head Quarters to send anyone in my condition out into the combat zone was a reckless decision! Dangerous for me and for the other guys in my infantry company!

A full infantry company has four platoons, each platoon divided into four squads of eight to ten men for a total of 130 to 160 infantrymen (or less due to deaths and wounds). An infantry company usually has to move in single file with one man chosen to lead the entire group. This man is referred to as the "point man." Obviously, that job is the most dangerous and is rotated throughout the company. Nobody wanted to be the first to encounter the many enemy dangers.

Early in my assignment with Charlie Company, it came time for our squad to share the point man duties. We happened to be heading into an area of small hamlets that was one of the nastiest Viet Cong strongholds in Vietnam. We called it "Pinkville." Its real name was My Lai...and it became the site of a terrible chapter in U.S. war history known as "The My Lai Massacre."

All of the experienced guys hated to have missions near My Lai. We were often catching sniper fire and tripping booby traps around the villages there...but we always found only civilians when we surrounded the area. We knew that the civilians were doing it but could never catch them in the act. By far, however, the worst part about operating in that area was the abundance of explosive booby traps on the trails surrounding the villages which often inflicted a dreaded loss of body parts. Walking point near My Lai was a nightmare!

Then, the day came for *my* turn to walk point. Soon after waking up that morning, my squadmates told me how horrible Pinkville was and that I'd better be more alert than I've ever been in my life! My biggest problem was that I still had pneumonia! I was weak, mostly deaf, and my head was full of mucus. "Be more alert than I'd ever been in my life?" Hell, I was barely functioning! I had a very bad feeling about the day ahead of me; the cloudy sky felt ominous.

Into our group strode our squad leader, Shorty, who had just come from the morning meeting with the officers and other squad leaders. "I'm walking point today," he announced.

Everyone knew that Shorty's presence increased *everyone's* chances of survival. So, when he made his bold declaration to walk point, everyone protested loudly. "No way, Shorty! It's not your turn at point!" Gesturing toward me, one blurted, "It's *his* turn; let him take point!" I felt the knot in my stomach tighten even more.

"No, you know how tricky this area is," Shorty said calmly but firmly. "Whoever walks point here needs to have a lot more experience than Twiggy has. Plus you know how sick he is. I'm taking point, and that's it."

I hated that I was miserably ill in a combat zone, but I couldn't help but feel incredible relief to hear Shorty's order. I knew that my senses and mental sharpness were severely compromised. I also knew that I would eventually get well and that my time would come soon enough. But for that day, I would follow Shorty's lead on point as our Charlie Company moved out on the dry, brushy, winding trail toward My Lai.

With the immediacy of the moment in mind and in preparation for my eventual turn as point, I tried to clear my foggy mind for every possible clue of danger along the trail. My next memories are a horrible blur. Not long after we had trekked along the trail, there was a loud flashing boom in front of me! I was blasted with heavy debris and instinctively jerked my face downward to be shielded by my helmet. When I could look up, I saw a cloud of smoke and dust mushrooming above the bushes ahead. Shorty had hit a booby-trap!

The next thing I remember was all of us huddling around our fallen squad leader with smoke still around us in the air. Shorty had been horribly wounded. The heart-breaking sight on the ground before us was devastating! (As I now recount this horrible tragedy, it takes everything I have to hold my thoughts together. The searing memory pleads with my mind to banish the images into the blackness of my repression! But this heart-wrenching story needs to be told no matter *how* much it hurts.)

As the medic frantically worked on him, Shorty regained consciousness. There was deep anguish and dirt-streaked tears on everyone's faces. "HANG ON SHORTY," we choked! The booby trap, a rigged mortar round, had savaged Shorty's poor body! Realizing that he had been blinded by the blast, Shorty reached up to feel his eyes…only to discover that his hands were missing, too. The mournful wail that he let out will burn deep into my soul forever!

It didn't seem like *anything* in the world could possibly be worse… but I was soon proven wrong. After several heart-wrenching seconds of wailing at the reality of what he had lost, Shorty paused a moment then cried loudly in bitter anguish, "KILL ME…SOMEONE PLEASE KILL ME! If you care about me at all please don't let me live like this! Shoot me…please!!!"

We were horrified beyond horrified! We were being begged to kill our best friend. And we *understood* why! Shorty's worst nightmare was our worst nightmare! We all cried bitterly along with Shorty. I hate to say this, but some of us surely heard voices inside our heads screaming, "Do it for him! He's *begging* us! Do it for him...he can't do it himself without hands!" No one did it. No one *could*. Shorty was everybody's best friend! We couldn't do it. We condemned him to live.

I remember the summoned Medevac helicopter roaring up and away with Shorty aboard and the profound anguish on the ground below him turning to rage. Bitter eyes flashed from the vanishing Medevac to the village of My Lai! *Then*—in a bitter moment—one of Shorty's fellow seventeen survivors turned his angry eyes toward me!

"This was your booby-trap," he growled tightly, "not Shorty's! This was your day to walk point! That should be you on the chopper...*not Shorty!!!*" His words cut like a jagged knife! Guilt came crushing in on my pounding heart! Oh, how it hurt that I knew that he was right. Had I not been new and sick with pneumonia that *would* have been me being carried away on the helicopter!

Another of the seventeen survivors echoed an anguished agreement but then other guys saw what was happening and quickly thrust themselves into the exchange. "Hey! Shorty would've done the same for you guys too if you weren't able to walk point safely! That's the way Shorty was. He'd do it for *any* of us!" Everyone was understandably aching and enraged after having just seen the most respected, valued, and loved guy in the company destroyed. Someone else yelled, "Yeah, it was those gook sons-of-bitches that set the booby-trap!" Rage was quickly redirected toward the Pinkville village. In the heat of our intense bitterness and pain, the horrible My Lai Massacre might easily have happened right then instead of a few weeks later. "Wiping out that whole damn Viet Cong village" crossed the lips of several men! I was no longer the target of rage, but a *lifetime* seed of guilt had nevertheless been planted. I've never gotten over that day.

As time passed, I became physically strong and healthy...and *hardcore!* Be it consciously or unconsciously, I had a deep need to make up for the tragic loss of a true war hero and friend. I became every bit as tough and competent as the seasoned "old-timers." I *had* to be...many tough battles lie ahead.

The original core of seventeen survivors included only one officer—a hard-as-nails first lieutenant who was extremely combat savvy. With our company having so many new guys, including new officers, this first lieutenant campaigned to reorganize our company. To give us the best chance of survival, he talked the company commander into letting him lead a small platoon of only fifteen or so men who would always walk point for the whole company. These few men would then be rotated on point every 15 days…thus giving the company's point men much more experience than with the original model. The fifteen men in this small "point platoon" would closely share information and their experiences with one another to create an unusually well-trained team of point men referred to by the lieutenant as his Recon group—short for reconnaissance. I became a member of this team for my remaining months in Charlie Company, 2/1, 196th Infantry Brigade.

Later, after having transferred to the 11th Brigade's 4th Battallion of the 21st Infantry Regiment, I became a squad leader in its Delta Company. I modeled myself after Shorty. I often took point in the tough situations. Forty years later, in 2003, I entered the reception room of that infantry company's first reunion. Old platoonmates were standing around the registration table trying to recognize me as I walked toward them. Forty years of age, silver hair, and a thick set of Harley whiskers had changed me from my boyish Vietnam days' "Twiggy" looks, prompting quizzical expressions of "who is this guy?!" Then one of them blurted, "It's Twig! You're the one who always wanted to walk point!" Yes, I thought, but I was the squad leader point man who went home *whole*.

Shorty, my friend and hero, I don't know if you are still alive, but this chapter is written in your honor! I'm eternally grateful for your heroic and selfless sacrifice. You will, forever, be *The Soldier's Soldier*.

TWO HEARTS RACING

Introduction

"TWO HEARTS RACING" IS A POEM about the unexpected meeting of two young soldiers from opposing sides in the Vietnam War in 1968. Both were newly recruited into combat, and were naturally fearful of that time when they would eventually encounter the dreaded enemy. On a warm day, with streams of sunlight angling down through the green canopy of a remote mountain jungle, that dreaded time was about to arrive.

By unusual circumstance, both of them were momentarily apart from their fellow troops. One, a lone young North Vietnamese soldier, had apparently been sent down to the lowlands to get rice for his unit and was returning with two full baskets slung on his back. The other soldier, a young GI only ten day afield, was laying exhausted against a rocky outcrop which he had found a few feet off a main trail on which his infantry company had stopped for a break.

Then, a slight sound from the other side of the rocks caused the young GI to twist around, only to be startled to see an enemy soldier just twenty yards away! Both momentarily froze in their tracks...mouths agape and young eyes wide open!

Both were well-armed soldiers, but innocent eyes revealed that gentle, boyish spirits lived beneath their layers of battle gear. Fate had suddenly placed them face-to-face with no one else in sight...just the two of them alone.

There are many heart-warming scenarios that could be imagined in a unique situation like this. The following poem, "Two Hearts Racing," was written by me—that young American infantryman who happened to meet that young North Vietnamese soldier in 1968. The life-changing event that happened on that warm sunny day is told on the following page.

Two Hearts Racing
Robert Jewell, U.S. Infantry 1968-1969

The Draft Board had ordered
That you fight a war;
Sweet, peaceful childhood
Is gone evermore.
They've sent you to Asia—
Ten light-years from home—
You have to survive, now,
This green battle zone.

Your first day has ended;
No Cong were around.
Then comes the nighttime
Without rifle sound.
Your eyes peer, you taste fear,
White knuckles grip gun;
You lay there and pray there:
"God, thanks for Day One."

Then ten more days quiet,
You're feeling less tight;
Your guard's dropping lower,
"This jungle's alright!"
It seems not as bad
As you feared it would be,
"The battles are elsewhere,
From harm you'll be free."

But then—Without warning—
Young Cong, face-to-face!
He's shocked just like you...

Two hearts start to race!
Eternal time passes—
Both frozen by fright—
He's first into action,
But turns and takes flight!

Your well-drilled mind reacts:
Raise rifle from your knees,
Aim and shoot—without thought—
Dear God, with too much ease!
The peaceful air explodes
With piercing rifle "Cracks!"
Hot missiles slice through leaves
And pound a young man's back!
Young flesh tears, legs give way;
Yon soldier is soaked in red!
Pleading soul implores him: "Rise!...
Safe cover is just ahead!!!"
Your killing metal pummels on
—No mercies in your gun—
Your deadly, *dead-on* stream of fire
Destroys his desperate run.

Again the air falls silent...
Young Cong is silent too...
Only *one* heart races now—
That heart pounds *hard* in you!
Up ahead, on the ground,
Red blood is flowing bright;
Shattered life drains away...
Young soul, torn loose, takes flight.

War-mates gather 'round you
And slap you on the back,
"Hail warrior," they proclaim,
"You have that killer knack!"
But why, then...if that's true,
Does your young heart ache?
Could it be, this pain in you
Reveals a warrior *fake?*

Northward, in *the land of Minh,*
A mother waits in vain,
Praying that her soldier boy
Will soon be home again.
Her vigil light, that hopeful light,
Will soon be snuffed out cold—
When, Army message at her door:
The dreaded news is told.

Bloody war enslaves your days
And shows you horrid sights;
Darkness holds you hostage, too:
That mother haunts your nights.
Fitful dreams replay her cries,
Your conscience cannot rest!
Her dead son's photo, wet with tears,
Pressed tightly to her breast.

Epilogue

No, a romantic heart-warming scenario did not actually happen that day. My gentle nature was trumped by my intense combat training, and a sad reality of war prevailed. My training for combat was brutally tough—as combat training needs to be. Nations must provide for their defense. In the process, the war machine often takes gentle young men like me...and turns them into "tightly structured units" that will deliver death upon request.

My fateful encounter in the jungle remains ingrained in my mind. The young NVA soldier was carrying a loaded, brand-new Russian SKS-44 assault rifle. However, upon seeing me, as described in my poem, he made a decision to drop his rice-packs and flee for his life (perhaps there just wasn't any killer inside of him). Anyway, he had only gotten about forty yards away before I set myself and mechanically opened up on him—one deadly-aimed shot at a time.

I could tell that my bullets were hitting him, but still he ran! I continued shooting and he soon fell. In seconds, however, he arose and scrambled onward toward a shielding crest only fifteen yards ahead on his path. Again I resumed shooting until he fell beside the trail a second time. To my great dismay, he got up yet again! I couldn't believe it! My heart of hearts desperately wanted my shooting to end...but he more desperately wanted to escape. And I did as I was trained: I continued pulling the trigger until he dropped for the third and final time.

My M-16 rifle had been hyped to be a deadly weapon, so I was shaken that it took so *many* shots to end it. But I was much more shaken that I had just killed someone! Meanwhile, my platoon quickly secured the area, and fellow soldiers soon gathered around his body—rifling through his clothes and equipment...with me, standing there in a thinly masked shock, looking down at what *looked* like a fifteen-year-old boy! Handsome, innocent-faced...and dead.

The fact that his ID papers gave his age to be nineteen consoled me little. To me, I had just shot a kid! Someone's son. In the back. Several times. My pounding heart felt sick—not proud. Platoonmates reassured me that the North Vietnamese soldier would have lived to kill American soldiers later if I had not killed him first. That was probably true; but nevertheless, the image of his young face stayed with me for many days. I can see him still.

Soon, however, the hardness of war numbed my compassion, and I succumbed to the "Sgt. Rock" mentality of my embattled infantry company. Within months I morphed into a bloodthirsty "hired gun"—complete with "notches" on my M-16 rifle (small stick figures of Cong which I drew on the stock of my gun). By the time I had finished fourteen months in combat, I had experienced more terror, gore, and violence than I could ever have imagined in the innocent, carefree days of my youth. I had changed. (Decades later, this change is exactly what my sweet mother saw when she tearfully lamented that her son that she had seen off to war never really came home.)

Upon my return from Vietnam, the Army offered me some days of "readjustment time." I declined. The only thing I wanted was to be a civilian again at the soonest possible minute. Just let me scrub the bloodstains from my hands and put the war far behind! I naively believed that I could do that. What I didn't know at that time, however, was that a mountain of horrors had been indelibly etched in the darkest depths of my subconscious mind. And while the powers of repression would allow me to function exceptionally well for the next couple of decades, the reality was that, for me, the war would *never* be entirely over.

I wrote "Two Hearts Racing" in 1987, about twenty years after I had ended the life of that young NVA soldier in Vietnam. I penned it only minutes after I had finished being a volunteer client for a practice counseling session that was part of a fellow student's counseling degree program requirements at Montana State University. I thought that I should at least make his practice session interesting, so I decided to talk about killing that young soldier. It was the first time I'd ever discussed any combat since returning from war! Because I had not yet displayed any mental problems from my Vietnam experience(s), I had anticipated that I could relay the story calmly and with ease. However, hugely intense emotions roared to life as the trained student counselor steered me into my *feelings* about the event! The enormity of emotions caught me totally off guard and absolutely overwhelmed my mind! What I had thought was going to be a casual practice counseling session instead turned my mind into a maelstrom! I had unwittingly opened *Pandora's Box!!!*

I was practically hyperventilating afterward as I left the counseling lab room. I soon found myself back in my dorm room, frantically pacing back and forth...trying to figure out how in the *hell* I was going to get that powerful Pandora back into her box! It was *critical* that I regain the clear mind that would be required by the rigorous Master's Degree program that I had just begun.

With war images flashing vividly in my head, the rhythmic beat of a military drum seemed to pound with each step of my pacing feet. Strangely, this rhythm began to intertwine with my thoughts until the tormenting images took the form of poetic verse. Though never one to write poetry, I felt strongly compelled to sit and write out my feelings. I scribbled as fast as I could and the poem "just blurted itself out of my heart!" It took only about thirty minutes to complete.

Upon finishing the poem, I put my head down on the desk and cried like a little child, with heavy tears wetting the words I had just written. It was the first time that I cried about anything since I was a young boy. Decades of unconscious imprisonment in a secret dark world of guilt and horror was finally unlocked in a flurry of writing and a flood of tears.

Writing "Two Hearts Racing" was a huge catharsis, and it freed my mind for the rigors of my Master's Degree. However, with the drying of my tears came the disconcerting revelation that repressed emotions and memories of war lurked hidden inside me. Ever since returning from war, I worked hard "to be okay" again...and I truly believed that I had succeeded in making myself okay. But I *wasn't* okay and Pandora was not dead! My cathartic poem had merely sung her back to sleep. Pandora was reawakened in 1995, reborn via an extraordinarily stressful year. Subsequent life-saving therapy returned most of my function, but it appeared (and appears) that full healing will probably never happen in my lifetime. Nevertheless, I will never give up trying "to be okay" again. I have to...for the sake of my *still*-racing heart.

REVERENCE FOR THE VICTIM

A COUPLE DAYS HAD PASSED since I had killed the young North Vietnamese soldier. Because he'd been carrying two large pack-baskets of rice, which were obviously intended for many, my company had been spending the last two days searching the network of mountain trails for the soldier's NVA camp.

My recollection of what happened during those days of search is compromised. My mind was in a state of shock by having just killed a human being, and I was still battling exhaustion from pneumonia. As such, I was wading through a mental fog that prevented me from keeping track of where we were and where we had traveled in relation to my fallen victim.

It was mid-morning and my company had paused on one of the trails we had been searching. Sunlight poured down where I stood, hunched over to take some of my infantry pack's heavy weight off of my sore shoulders. A squadmate, who was trekking in front of me, suddenly said to me, "Hey, Montana, here's your gook!" I looked up in bewilderment!

Pete, the squadmate, was a few feet off the trail where he had spotted the body of an NVA soldier and was standing over the body, which was momentarily hidden from my view by low-growing vegetation. "Here he is," he said "come look at him!" I felt a tightness in my stomach and a reluctance to believe what he was telling me; this setting didn't seem right. Nevertheless, I headed over to view his find.

Upon arriving where Pete stood grinning as he leaned on a walking stick that he had picked up along the trail, I was shocked and filled with disgust when I looked down to see a grotesquely bloated corpse covered with flies! It hardly looked like a human being let alone that same handsome, boyish young soldier whose life I had taken two days earlier! My innocence begged me to look away, but I couldn't! I couldn't resist the need to search that horribly swollen face for any sign of resemblance. I found none at all. "This ain't the one I killed," I argued in disgust…adamantly denying Pete's claim! "This ain't even the same place!"

Mind you, it *was* actually the same young NVA soldier I had killed. The body was so horribly disfigured from the ravages of tropical heat and humidity that he was unrecognizable to me. And it *was* the same place. I hadn't realized that we were on the same trail where I had shot the young soldier because we had been traveling on it from the *opposite* direction. This reverse perspective of the trail, plus the different lighting, made the setting look very different. Also, my memory of the killing scene was mostly etched as a tunnel vision image of his lifeless young body lying in the late afternoon shadows as my fellow GI's rummaged through his pockets and pack.

My psychologically restricted memory had convinced me that Pete was totally mistaken! "Yes it is," insisted Pete, pointing downhill on the trail ahead, "Don't you remember? You shot him from right down there!" I looked down the trail and was surprised to indeed see the mound from where I was shooting! Pete, noting that I had recognized the site of my shooting position, reaffirmed, "See, this is your gook!"

Still feeling some disbelief because this body looked so different, I started to walk away. I turned back around to look at his face once again. To my horror, I saw Pete stabbing his walking stick into the fly-covered eyes of the body!!! "It's your gook alright…hee, hee, hee!" Pete's mind had been completely indoctrinated by our infantry training's dehumanization of the Vietnamese (to make it easier to kill them)!

Aghast, I immediately stiffened into a tight bolt! "Stop that," I screamed. Pete should have recognized the great *intensity* of my alarm, but it sailed right over his head. "It's all right," he continued, *amused* at my reaction, "He's dead…see?!" and then took a couple more stabs into the fallen soldier's lifeless eyes! My heart jumped out of my chest and my horror flashed to absolute rage. With the speed of a blazing lightning bolt, I whirled and pounced at Pete, thrusting the aimed barrel of my M-16 rifle right at the middle of his extremely shocked face! "Get away from him!!" I growl-hissed with fiery rage sizzling through my clenched teeth.

Pete sprung away from the body like a shot. His eyes were popped wide in fear and shock; his tan face turned white! And wisely so! My eyes must have been flashing red...the wild eyes of a dangerous, *crazy* man! My mind was extremely distressed from having just killed a human being for the first time, and my sorrow and guilt was *much* more intense than *either* of us had understood! To my hypersensitive mind, Pete was committing an unbearably violent and disrespectful violation of another human be-ing...of *my* victim who was lying dead because of me...*my* responsibility!

Pete instantly blurted in a very shaken, fearful voice, "Jesus, Mon-tana!!!" He took a couple quick steps back and a very purposefully flung his stick away to eliminate any further provocation of my very shocking, unexpected wrath! "Take it easy! Lower your weapon, Montana!...Geez, you're crazy, man! I wasn't hurting anything...he's *dead*. Calm down, man! Jesus!!!"

Seeing the fear and hurt in Pete's eyes, I felt the rapid return to my senses! My heart still pounding, I took a deep breath...and lowered my rifle...all the way down. Pete, still shaking, repeated, "Jesus!...Jesus, Montana!"

That extremely unpredictable, crazy moment had found me teeter-ing on the edge of a cliff...with my rifle pointed between the eyes of one of my own men! I was only slightly less shaken than Pete. I was both shocked and embarrassed at my wild reaction!

Of course, as soon as I regained some semblance of calm, I apolo-gized to Pete and tried to explain my reaction. He simply couldn't have known the intense, volatile remorse that I had been feeling from having just killed what looked like a mere boy! Pete and I were both frighten-ingly aware that I could have shot him dead in that tragic out-of-control situation—a situation which he truly believed was nothing more than an insensitive and harmless act.

Our company started moving forward again. I'd visibly eased Pete's mind—at least to the point that he wasn't worrying that I might still "plug him in the back"—but he was still rattled. Later, during our break for lunch, I explained more fully how horrible I felt about killing someone who seemed like only a kid…just like *us*…and a kid who had parents just like *our* parents who were agonizing for their son's safe return. I made a strong point that I was painfully aware that the young NVA's parents would never see *their* son again because of me! Yes, this was a war that we were in, but I was not yet hardened. My remorse had explosively compelled me to a ferocious defense of the sanctity of their son's body.

Although my unexpected reaction had surprised me too, at least it made sense to me. To a lesser extent it made sense to Pete too; at minimum, at least our discussion put us *on the same team* again. I'm eternally grateful that Pete wisely chose to back off as quickly as he did. Life prevailed this time, but dear God, I saw how easily horrible tragedies can occur in war zones! Human life is so fragile, especially when you have overstressed, heavily armed young men—boys really—in a war zone!

At the present time, decades after my soul-searching discussion with Pete in the jungles of Vietnam, I've taken special time to write about that event because I'm still fascinated by my near-lethal reaction over a *dead body.* It is an interesting phenomenon to me; I was protecting my victim's lifeless body! It seems almost *absurd*…shooting someone to death, and then be willing to protect his lifeless body at immense cost! But I did just that.

I'm left with an intriguing concept: taking a human life is actually an extremely intimate act! Only giving life to a human in birth is equally intimate. I believe that both acts are strikingly related: one act leads life into our physical world, and the other leads life back out. One thing I do know for certain: I will always feel an extraordinarily (and heartbreakingly) intimate bond with my young NVA victim. Our spirits are forever connected.

TOUGHENED

BEFORE BEING DRAFTED, I had been a wiry, quick, and strong-for-my-size kid with natural fighting instincts, so in military training I loved the calisthenics that pushed us to our limits. While most of the guys groaned and whined, I was "eating it up," and was occasionally chosen to get up in front of my platoon to lead those calisthenics which were usually led by a buffed drill sergeant.

Infantrymen need to be tough, both physically and mentally. Military training is designed to forge that toughness. Following basic training, we who were assigned to infantry, entered infantry advanced individual training. Infantry AIT was especially tough and violent. It included learning to fight with our bayonets attached to our rifles. In that training, we had to attack a dummy enemy soldier, "a lunge-stab to his heart, a butt stroke into his crotch, and then a bayonet slash down across his neck"…all while loudly screaming "KILL!!!" I performed it like a savage animal! I loved being tough and the drill sergeants approved out loud. AIT's intensity and regular cruel abuse by the drill sergeants often seemed like outright sadism to us. Their goal, however, was actually to toughen us up for the *far* worse super-human physical demands and vicious cruelty of combat, which was only *weeks* away!

In my first week with my infantry company in Vietnam, I was given the nickname "Twiggy." One of the tough seventeen survivors, the one with most of his voice box shot out, light-heartedly commented that my very long eyelashes reminded him of the famous long-eyelashed British model, Twiggy. The comment got some chuckles and the nickname stuck. Dang, I thought, "Twiggy" was certainly not any kind of tough-guy nickname. But, perhaps that was fitting, especially since I had been battling a bad case of pneumonia during my first two to three weeks in Vietnam, which had left me in a very weakened, frail, and "less than tough" condition.

After finally regaining my health, though, I grew to be perhaps the toughest guy in my company—proven by two quick victories in fist-fights against larger, known-to-be-tough opponents. One of those fist fights was against an obnoxious-acting black guy in a base camp bar, and it came close to erupting into a black against white free-for-all... another story for me to write. My toughness, inside and out, gained me respect and was probably one of the factors in my being designated a Squad Leader so soon...despite my "Twiggy" looks.

My first infantry company was a *high-octane* lesson on being *brutally* tough! Charlie company's core of seventeen survivors demonstrated it loud and clear, fighting with a vicious rage and a cold heartlessness... a true love of killing! No mercy, just hate! The recent severe losses of nearly all of their squadmates hardened their hearts to stone. There was no longer any way to tell that they once may have been normal, happy kids before the war.

In the beginning, I was aghast at the most vicious examples of their savagery. But within two weeks, I had seen several of my mates killed or horribly maimed...and I quickly morphed into one of the rage-filled savages. This transition seemed to be an automatic, almost normal change. I found myself lusting for killing. That lust became a sick badge of honor when I, like the Old West gunslingers, was "carving notches" on my gun for kills that I had made.

My "kill notches" were actually inked stick figures of Vietnamese holding rifles. I drew them boldly on strips of green sticky-back tape that I pulled from packs of C-rations. I'd wrapped the tape tightly around some of the hard-plastic parts of my M-16...a perfect canvas for my carvings.

As a "code of honor," I restricted each stick figure to a kill that I was certain that only I had made." I killed countless enemy soldiers in combat—many more than the notches drawn on my M-16. But most of the time, I was able to shoot or throw grenades only at rifle flashes in dense foliage. As a consequence, it was often an unknown as to whether or not my kill attempt had been successful. Certainly some of those situations resulted in enemy deaths but, again, "my code of honor" dictated *confirmed* kills only. I had seven "confirmed kill notches" lined up on my green tape. At the end of my tour of duty, I had to return my M-16 ("my best friend") to the battalion armory. I'm sure that the GI's who checked weapons into the armory had conversation about my "notches."

My gung-ho attitude exposed me to greater danger than was normal for an infantryman…like my taking point man duty whenever I could in the most dangerous situations. Doubtlessly, that was because "Shorty" (my first squad leader) heroically sacrificed himself to walk point in my place when I was sick with pneumonia. That horrible event was a huge part of the hardening of my heart. My company suffered many more deaths and maiming injuries during my time in combat. Each time, the sweet boy of my youth was driven further into the past.

I kept a softness for the Vietnamese civilians, though—even protecting them from my own guys on several occasions. However, my hard attitude was deadly for enemy soldiers. Other than my first-time kill, the only time in which I killed an enemy and felt a twinge of humanity was when I was part of a combat assault with armored vehicles. We had been blasting our way forward when I happened to look back and saw a hole that was apparently the rear entrance to an enemy bunker. Something told me that I needed to quickly check it out before continuing on. Sneaking back, I sprang to the front of the bunker's "shooting window" with my M-16 aimed inside and ready to blaze away at any enemy that we might have missed when we blasted our way past.

My hunch was right, there was one alive, sprawled against the back of the bunker. Wounded and surprised by my return, he raised an open palm toward my deadly aimed M-16 and murmured something in Vietnamese—probably "You don't need to shoot, I'm mortally wounded." For a moment I thought that I should leave him. But I blazed away.

The final fleeting pain in his eyes caused my heart to feel a sharp slice. But I was lagging behind our combat assault, so I gritted my teeth, and quickly explained to my heart that I had done the right thing. After all, he may have healed to fight again. I "put the killing away" and sprinted back to the battle line. As I now describe this kill, I realize that my heart had been sliced deeper than I thought. I was, and still am, deeply affected by this. It makes me realize that, beneath the hard armored skin that I'd grown, the sweet boy of my youth had never totally left at any time.

So, what does toughness earn in combat? Sometimes survival, sometimes getting killed early, sometimes a promotion, and sometimes a valor medal on your chest. That "valor thing" sometimes makes me scoff. For sure, there were many acts of even profound valor in that war. But some non-combat GI's got Bronze Stars for doing nothing other than what many of us infantrymen did dozens of times. I performed acts of valor that deserved Bronze Stars—even by infantry standards, but I was never presented with one. I was, however, awarded the Army Commendation Medal, which is a degree lower than Bronze Stars. All valor medals are to be given *"for valor above and beyond the call of duty."* Therein lies the rub. Infantrymen regularly go into blazes of bullets to engage the enemy or to bail each other out, etc. Such actions are not defined as *beyond* call of duty for infantry; it's our *normal* duty. However, if a pilot, chaplain, truck driver, etc. did the same thing, he might be awarded a Bronze Star, Silver Star, Distinguished Service Medal, or even a Medal of Honor...because it is beyond *their* call of duty.

Also working against me was the fact that I got on the bad side of a new platoon leader right away. That misfortune happened when I, as a very experienced squad leader, had taken point-man duty on a trail that ran along the right side of a fairly wide river. Several miles into our trek, I suddenly spotted a large troop of enemy who were several hundred yards ahead on the point of a river bend. I radioed this to my platoon leader who came forward to take a look. We pulled back into cover where that new platoon leader, a 2nd lieutenant, called a huddle of the platoon sergeant, me, and our platoon's other three squad leaders. We all looked down at the lieutenant's topography map, which he laid out on the ground. As point-man, who leads the whole company along trails, I had been carefully following every detail of my own copy of the same map. The lieutenant announced that he would be calling an artillery strike on the enemy, and put his finger on the target area on the map. My eyes widened because I saw that he was actually pointing to the wrong point, the river point where *we* were currently positioned!

Normally, an officer's word is not to be disputed, but I had to speak up! Respectfully, but with the strong conviction required in this situation, I said, "Excuse me, Sir, but you are pointing to where we are now." He slowly looked up with a hard glare and replied tersely, "You don't think I know how to read a map, Sgt. Jewell?!" I felt very uncomfortable, but my closer study of the map confirmed to myself that indeed I was seeing our map correctly. As tactfully as possible, I pointed out the strong similarities between our river's point on the river and the enemy's point, and that the similarity created understandably confusing reference points. "At ease, Sargent!" he interrupted coldly! But I couldn't back down; his misreading the map would lead to a devastating artillery attack on our whole company! Looking at the map again, I persisted, "But Sir, look there's a little stream on the other side of the river's bend, just before the point where you're targeting. That inlet sharply angles forward into the river, making it hard to see as it's passed. But I *did* look back and noted it as we passed it a few minutes ago! Now look at the river's point where those dinks are...there's *no matching inlet* in the bend across from them! The point with the stream inlet has to be where *we* are!"

The young lieutenant was clearly steamed, but I spoke so convincingly that he looked back to his map. It was a tense moment for everyone in the huddle! Then, the older, very respected veteran Platoon Sergeant who had been scrutinizing the map during my description, spoke up with a gentle deference, "Sir, I too remember seeing that little inlet about 200 yards back...I think Sgt. Jewell is correct; that's the bend where we are." All of us studied the map closer for stream inlets. The facts were soon clear. The lieutenant didn't look up from his map and said quietly, "You better be right, Sgt. Jewell. And there doesn't need to be any later discussion about this from any of you." The lieutenant's last comment was an implicit command, not a suggestion.

Artillery was eventually called in, and it was on the enemy soldiers. I shut up about that incident, but the young platoon leader had felt humiliated in front of the other leaders of his platoon. Thereafter, there was always an undertone of coldness whenever he and I had communication and any valorous acts that I did were viewed with indifference by him (this man who had to okay all valor citations for his platoon). Surely he felt deep relief that my actions stopped him from getting his own men killed—a tragedy and a career-ending disaster. But the lieutenant held a grudge.

I have a poor sense of the chronology of my Vietnam events. I really can't be sure whether any of my clear acts of valor happened while under that lieutenant, but I do know that a couple of the men in my squad would call me Sgt. Rock (the comic book U.S. Army hero). So I probably did do things that were "above and beyond the call of duty" while that lieutenant was my platoon leader.

There are two valorous examples that I can remember. One is described later in my "Moment Of Death" chapter, when I volunteered to be the initial "tunnel rat" to slide down a small hole that was the entrance to an extremely "fresh" (occupied or booby-trapped) underground NVA camp!

The other happened one day when most of our platoon was attacked as they passed through a large clearing on our trail. Men who hadn't already been killed were pinned down behind very meager cover—a few rocks, stumps, etc. Two enemy machine gunners were shooting through very small slots at the base of an abandoned French-era stone building that was up-slope from that clearing. Everything in front of the enemy's stone fortification was lethally open, and everywhere else behind and to the sides of the building was surrounded by impenetrable jungle. The circumstances gave the enemy great protection as well as a perfect "killing field" of everything in the wide clearing down in front of them.

I was just out of the line-of-fire on the dense trail along with a few guys including our then platoon leader. We were trying to figure a way to stop the enemy gunners. There was no apparent solution to the problem; the NVA machine gunners mowed down everything that moved!

Then I remembered that a dry, seasonal streambed crossed our trail about thirty yards back. I trotted back to look at it closer. It appeared to extend up close to the left side of the enemy fortification. The streambed was overgrown but not *impenetrable*. I hustled back to the lieutenant and described it. I suggested that one of us with a LAW (a telescoping single shot, bazooka-like weapon) might be able to crawl unseen up through that streambed's undergrowth and get close enough to accurately blast through the enemy's stone wall slots. The lieutenant listened to my plan and then said, "Are you volunteering?"

Minutes later, I had our company's one LAW slung around my neck and was beginning my low crawl up the shallow streambed. The streambed's overgrowth created a maze of thorny bushes with snaggy branches growing from their bases. Lots of dry leaves and twigs lined the bottom—a perfect home for every spider, centipede, and scorpion in Asia and whatever varieties of poisonous snakes might also be lounging there! I felt like I was entering Satan's basement! "Dear God," I prayed, "Let those critters scram the hell out of the way as I belly-crawl through their crappy home!" But thwarting my efforts of shooing critters away, was the more pressing need to crawl quietly!

The streambed started out about five feet deep but grew steadily shallower uphill. My crawl was fraught with stabs by branches and thorns—a gauntlet of troublesome snags that constantly grabbed at my fatigues! Given the dangers that my platoon was currently suffering, I moved as fast as I could, but I also needed to move "invisibly slow" and quietly enough that my approach wouldn't catch the eyes or ears of the enemy too soon. Each few yards of gain meant that the streambed's increasing shallowness was slowly removing my cover, but I was now getting so close! Every tiny snap of a twig and every movement of a branch threatened to alert the enemy of my presence! A loud thought was pounding inside my head, "What the *shit* am I getting myself into?!"

The tight, spiny spaces that I had been squeezing through would in *no* way allow me to turn around at that point. The only way out of this shitty mess was forward…and my dry streambed was now only about eighteen inches deep! I had already managed to get within shooting range, about 130 feet away from the building by then. I had desperately been trying to find a spot where I could open the telescoping LAW, lowly kneel, aim, and accurately shoot! But the undergrowth was too dense!

In just a few feet, I would run out of landscape. I was forced to open the LAW in a crappy tight space! Then, exposed to the enemy, I had to *slowly* finagle the three foot-long weapon through the branches to try to get it pointed toward the building. But, because of such dense branches all around me, I couldn't get the LAW angled downward enough to hit the narrow gunners' slots! *Damn* it! The best I could do was to hit the building about five feet above the enemy gunners.

Shit!!! This plan didn't work out as perfectly as I had envisioned when I was safely down on the trail! I didn't like my chances of success. It was very unlikely that the blast of my LAW's missile, hitting several feet over the enemy's heads, would kill them—but they sure as hell would know I was less than 100 feet away then! Firing my LAW was going to produce a fiery, bazooka back-blast that could easily set fire to whence I came! One final prayer: "Dear God, please give my platoon enough serious firepower to keep the enemy from *killing my ass* after I shoot! Amen."

I took a deep breath, squeezed the trigger, and..."BOOOOM!!!" Almost immediately I heard the second "BOOM!" of the missile's explosion against the wall. I flattened myself tight against the streambed to be as invisible as possible to the soon-to-come bullet retaliation from the enemy. My position was now fully highlighted by the smoke from my LAW's double-ended blast!

The first thing to immediately concern me inside my smoky cloud was feeling burning twig cinders on the backs of my legs. Damn! But at least the smoke might keep the enemy from seeing me slapping out cinders. Intense shooting erupted from GI M-16's below and welcome blasts of GI grenades exploded up at the enemies' fortification! I felt hope that the LAW blast opened a hole big enough to produce a lethal vulnerability from GI grenades. Nevertheless, enemy bullets soon sprayed the branches above my body! I was just *barely* low enough to avoid getting hit!

The battle eventually ended, but everything that followed—everything after the enemy's bullets chopping branches just above my flattened body—got repressed by my mind. The only thing that I can remember is my feeling like a failure that I couldn't get a clean shot at the little slots from which the enemy fired their guns. I don't even remember if my platoon killed the enemy gunners or if the enemy fled out the back of the building and escaped.

Nevertheless, my action was certainly "above and beyond the call of duty" danger! Yes, it could also be described as damned youthful *foolhardiness,* but I can't recall how it was judged at the time. I received no Bronze Stars at any time in Vietnam, so maybe this action was judged to have failed somehow or was downplayed by that begrudging lieutenant.

Everything beyond what I have just written about that event is repressed, so I don't know. Damn it! No matter what the platoon leader's determination was, I would still like to know how my plan and action were judged. Damn the fickle valor awards too. I never felt I did anything worthy of earning a medal anyway; I just fought for my squadmates, and the civilians, and to keep myself alive. Writing about this event made me sick with adrenaline and anxiety, as I had to relive the event, and doing so left me frustrated at the military's not-always-fair system.

In the end, I was always the best soldier that I could be, and I'm proud of my service. I served with honor, loyalty, and courage. As squad leader (Sgt. "Twig"), I led my men with integrity, well-honed skills, and interminable care for my squad and platoon. They regard me with true respect to this day. In recent years, a few of them got together in California. Days later, I received a package from them that contained a wad of the heaviest gauge of steel wool, a stiff-wired paint-scraper brush, and a note. The note read, "Twig's Toilet Paper."

I left the war zone...toughened.

THE INFANTRYMAN'S NATURE WORLD

BEYOND BEING JUST A WAR ZONE TO ME, Vietnam was an extraordinarily beautiful country. I grew up in Montana with a great love for nature. Southeast Asia was new to me and stunning. The following are some of my most memorable and pleasant "nature experiences" during my time in Vietnam.

I was assigned to the 23rd U.S. Infantry Division, known as Americal Division. Our area of operation was the northernmost fourth of South Vietnam, known militarily as I Corps (eye kor). I Corps was about 50 miles wide by 200 miles long, bordered by the white beaches of the warm South China Sea to the east, Laos to the west, and our mysterious foe— North Vietnam—to the north.

The sandy beaches quickly rose to a lowland region of small, grass hut villages of farmers who had chickens, hogs, pineapple plants, coconut trees, and emerald green rice paddies. The agricultural lowlands then rose to great mountains that were covered by fabulous rain forests, which contained some of the world's richest variety of plants and wildlife, a biologist's paradise!

The Rice Paddy Villages Region

I have never seen anything as green as a rice paddy! Almost a glowing green! Rice grows in a swamp environment, and the Vietnamese created these swamps by building an impressive series of mud dikes that dammed the water for growing their rice. These amazing rice paddy terraces sometimes extended from the Laotian mountain region all the way to the South China Sea.

Vietnam's rice paddies are extremely fertile from the many nutrients that wash down from the jungles. The farm families continually added more nutrients by using the paddies as their toilets. Don't get too grossed out, though. Excrement was quickly broken down in the tropically heated water, and fecal bacteria were quickly consumed by a huge assortment of other microscopic organisms. These rice paddies are actually very thriving ecosystems that also included small fish that the Vietnamese catch to eat with their rice.

Vietnam in the late 1960's was not mechanized. Only the "better off" farmers owned the closest things to our farm machinery, water buffalos! These huge beasts were used as tractors to till paddies or carry heavy loads. I have fond mental images of young Vietnamese boys out in a rice paddy atop these broad backed beasts...sitting or casually lying like American boys do while on the floor watching TV. These little farm boys used a small stick "to steer" the beast with gentle taps. I wonder if those kids had to earn "driver's licenses."

Rice typically constituted about 90 percent of the farm family's diet. Yes, farms often had chickens and hogs, too, but I surmise that some of those farm animals were meant for sale, while some were probably stolen as rations by the North Vietnamese soldiers who traveled through the farmlands at night. Wild big game never seemed to be around these villages; such animals lived only in the jungles farther inland. Thus, the Vietnamese farm families, needing to add protein to their morning, noon, and night meals of rice, would add any protein that they had available.

I witnessed one of their meal preps one evening when my company had set up camp around a Cong besieged village. While I sat on the ground near a hut, heating my C ration dinner, a Vietnamese lady emerged from her hut carrying a large flat basket under one arm, and the family dog under her other arm. She nodded cordially at me as she walked past, and disappeared along a path into the nearby foliage. I imagined that she was going to do a chore with a neighbor and was taking her pet, Fido, along. An hour later, she returned with a wide smile on her face, and hoisting the big tray on her shoulder—now piled with dark red slabs of meat and a knife stuck into the slabs. Where was Fido? Fido was riding on the tray.

I also vividly remember another one of their protein sources! This one I saw when I was on a weapons search mission at a remote farm that was nestled at the jungle's edge. With me was a six- or seven-year-old Vietnamese boy, a "baby son," (pronounced "baby sahn"). The boy was tagging along with me as I headed out toward a grass roofed livestock pen in back. As I approached, I saw a large flat basket that appeared to contain boiling gray mud. I thought, "What the...?"

Arriving at the basket (think: three-foot-wide woven pizza pan), I was befuddled to see that the "boiling gray mud" was actually a dense mat of thousands of wiggling wormlike larva! It was obvious that this was being cultured—not accidentally occurring. Again I thought, with much greater puzzlement, *What the...?!!!"* I looked down at the boy and exclaimed, "Baby son, what is *this?*" He looked at me with a huge smile and twinkling eyes and said, while patting his tummy, "Chop-chop... *number one* chop-chop!" In Vietnamese/American Pidgin English, that means, "Food *yummy* food!" I later learned that Vietnamese will hungri-ly throw a handful of these mealworms *alive* into their bowl of rice and eat them. (Okay, baby son, thanks, but protein aside I want none of your "number one" chop-chop in *my* chop-chop C rations)!

The Fabulous Mountain Rainforests

Wow! My favorite place on Earth! Many times we were flown into the mile high mountain jungles to seek out NVA camps. I loved it! Montana has its beloved mountains; they aren't nearly as dense with plant and animal species as they are in Vietnam. Huge, lush trees with networks of vining plants woven among them occupied almost every inch of the jungle floor. Below the tallest tree canopies, grew another layer of slightly smaller trees, and below those trees grew yet *another* layer of trees, and, finally, growing on the rainforest floors, were super dense thickets of thousands of plant species.

Though the mountains were teeming with amazing varieties of animals, you would rarely see them because of the foliage density. The animals would always see *us* though. Southeast Asian rainforests are so dense that humans can travel through them only along "trail tunnels." These had to be constantly carved with machetes or the trails would grow shut in weeks! As an "oft time point man," I sliced many a trail. Sometimes trails would "slice back" because some of the vines were thickly covered with little thorns that turned vines into sharp saw blades if they rubbed against skin. Intense work and heat was involved in machete chopping through all those vines as a point man, so I usually switched my tough fatigue shirt for a thin sleeveless green undershirt. Coolness was chosen over skin protection. I remember emerging from one stint of point man duty looking like I'd been in a daylong knife fight!

Nevertheless, some of the memories of my time in those glorious mountain rainforests are my favorite. Here are some of those. *Warning: Some of these stories will make readers wonder if I was taking drugs. I wasn't.*

The Pea Pods

One day we were taking a break while ascending a steep boulder strewn mountain streambed. The stream carved out a narrow corridor view of the sky, with vines hanging high between trees that lined the streambed. As I lay across a big boulder, gazing mindlessly upward, my eyes suddenly focused on *huge pea pods* on one of the vines...I mean HUGE! I honestly estimate that the pods were about six feet long with bulges of cantaloupe size peas inside! I felt like I was in a "Jack and the Bean Stalk" fairytale. I took pictures with my Instamatic, but my camera was unfortunately lost later (explained in one of the subsequent chapters about getting tear-gassed in Vietnam). Lost along with that camera were undeveloped rolls, which contained amazing photos, plus invaluable pics of my now-forgotten Charlie Company squadmates in the 196th Infantry.

The Five-Foot Feather

One overcast morning, my company was in a valley busily loading an enormous amount of supplies into our packs for what was to be a long combat mission into the distant mountains. We were dismayed to hear our orders were to trek the twenty-three-kilometer distance (fifteen miles) with perhaps the heaviest packs we ever had (ninety lbs?) by 2 P.M.! Off we went, grumbling!

Later, within about six miles of our bivouac site, we were resting. One of the guys looked at the mountains of our destination and re-marked that there were several reconnaissance planes circling the top of the highest mountain. Someone scoped them with binoculars and ex-claimed, "Those aren't planes...those are birds!" "No way!" we all chimed, "Birds can't be that big!" Upon taking turns with the binoculars, we all affirmed that they were indeed birds, like condors, only much bigger! "Wow, man! I can't wait to see them when we get there!"

We never saw those birds when we got into those mountains. They likely spotted us and fled. However, I did find an incredible feather! By pure chance, while we had stopped for one of our pauses on a dark overgrown trail, I looked into the tangled foliage and spotted the feather a few feet off the trail. Spotting it was pure luck because the feather was mottled brown—camouflaged against the fallen dead leaves. I was so astounded by its size that, despite my heavy pack and aching shoulders, I took out my large K bar knife and cut my way to get it. Once retrieved, I brought it back to the trail, and my squadmates marveled at the sheer size of the feather with me!

A squadmate used my camera and took a photo of me holding the feather. I posed with the feather quill on the ground in front of me. Its tip reached my nose—easily a five-foot long flight feather! Tail feathers were much more narrow and not nearly as thick or stiff. Being a biology teacher after Vietnam, I studied photos of the world's largest birds: condor, albatross, and Marabou stork. Their longest wingspans are about ten to twelve feet and their wing feathers are about two and a half to three feet long. My feather must have come from a bird with a wingspan of about twenty feet! Such a monster is apparently one of the thousands of species that have *still* not been documented by scientists because such animals live deep in vast, roadless rainforests. I'd hate to think that "my birds" were members of a small group that have since become extinct due to man's habitat destruction and incursions! Or...maybe those birds still lurk deep in the dense mountains of the Vietnam Laotian border!

The Vine Prank

Another one of my favorite rain forest memories was on a very rugged ascent of a steep mountain switchback trail. At one point, I looked *straight down* at platoonmates who were 100 feet below me on this same trail where I had been minutes earlier. I was seeing them through a woven mesh of stout roots and vines that grew along the mountain trail at my feet. A crazy prank entered my mind. I got the attention of the guys below me, then said, "Catch!" and threw my body off into the vine mesh! It looked like I was going to fall the 100 feet down to them, but the vines firmly held like I had judged they would. Guys, both below and beside me, gasped! Some laughed, some scolded me for being crazy! But for me, I was just enjoying a mischievous boy's high adrenaline prank.

Glowing in the Dark

My very favorite mountain rainforest memory happened while on a night ambush. Earlier that day, my company had trekked past a place where a rocky stream cascaded down from the jungle mountainside and lightly flowed across our trail. The boulder lined sides of the stream looked like a sneaky pathway for enemy soldiers moving at night and, thus, a perfect site for us to set up a squad sized ambush that night. A mile or two past the stream, my company established its nightly bivouac camp. The company commander chose my squad to be the one to backtrack to that streambed to set up a night ambush site higher upstream. It was early night when our band of about eight men reached the stream crossing. We headed up its banks.

At some point up the streambed, we beheld a sight like no other. The rocks and ground along the stream were glowing light green! The stream, which looked like any other in daylight, had transformed into a luminescent wonderland in the dark! Water flowing over the rocks in the stream looked like flowing light! Each step of our boots on the ground and rocks showed as black silhouettes against the glowing light. It was surreal! The bushes and trees along the streambed were dark and we were dark. Only the winding, tumbling stream and bed were light!

I'm still in awe of that scene. There must have been immense colonies of phosphorescent bacteria, fungus, or lichens that dwelled along that very special streambed. I have ached to be able to return there again in peacetime. It was perhaps one of the most beautiful things I have seen in my life! That night's ambush? I have no idea…all I can remember is the glowing streambed.

WOUNDED IN ACTION

MY FIRST COMPANY HAD MORE THAN ITS SHARE of genuine hard-core tough guys! Their attitude when I first got there was extremely toxic, and it worsened every time more men died. Not too long after I arrived, I received my first wound—an inch-long bullet slice through the flesh on the side of my left knee. Another quarter inch inward, the bullet would have hit bone and exploded my knee joint. After the battle, the platoon sergeant came around to each squad as usual, to inquire about award recommendations. I was one to raise a hand for a Purple Heart. One of my company's seventeen hardcore survivors scanned my body and then asked, "Wounded? Where?"

Two small holes were in my fatigue pant leg. I pulled it up and exposed the slice. The other hardcore survivors, all of whom had *substantial* wounds from their earlier battles, guffawed, "You call that a Purple Heart?!" one of them said, "That's just a graze. You wait a little while and you'll earn a *real* Purple Heart!" Another one of them added, with a half grin, "Yeah, your momma might have to collect it for you after you're dead, but you'll earn a real one." I initially thought that his comment was an attempt at sick humor, but he was serious. The platoon sergeant, an "old" 30-something war-seasoned black guy, calmly dismissed their comments and said to me, "That's a bullet wound suffered in battle; it fully qualifies for a Purple Heart if you put in for it."

The other hardcores said nothing more, but just looked at me as if to say, "Well, punk?" I felt caught between standing up for my rights versus wanting to be respected by the older war dogs whose leadership was important to me. I looked at their grizzled faces for a few seconds...then looked back to the waiting platoon sergeant and said, "I guess not...I'll wait for a 'real' one."

It took three or four months before I qualified for a "real" Purple Heart. My company was on-line and out in the open, teamed with a battalion of 1st Cavalry APC's (Armored Personnel Carriers) for a combat assault on a large NVA force that massed around the village of Tam Ky. We infantrymen were spread between the APC's, which were blazing away with their machine guns and canon fire. Storms of bullets were flying in both directions! I was firing my M-16 at an enemy's rifle flashes in the trees when, suddenly, there was a long streak that traveled from an adjacent hillside to an APC that was a few feet away from me! The streak was a deadly RPG anti-tank rocket! The APC suddenly turned into an extremely bright white flash of light with an instantaneous BOOOOM!!! For what felt like seconds, it seemed like I was floating...then felt myself crunching into the ground onto my right shoulder!

The next thing I remember were my squadmates quickly gathering up my helmet and rifle and hauling me to the protective cover of a nearby bomb crater. My Oklahoma buddy, Gary "Pokey Okie" Perry, who half carried me to the cover, was beside me. "Are you okay, Twig?" he drawled. I was still a little fog-headed as I tried to appraise my situation, "I...think so." But, as I turned my head while answering, I could feel a distinct dangling from my left ear! "Oh shit," I thought, "My ear has nearly been blown off!"

"My ear!" I exclaimed with a grimace to Pokey! My Oklahoma buddy looked at the side of my head and reached over to the side of my head, saying—to my horror—"Oh, here, let me get rid of that for you." I was aghast that my friend was intending to tear off the rest of my ear! "No!" I cried, trying to stop him! But I was too late; he'd already gotten a hold and pulled! I felt a firm tug and heard a ripping sound! "Damn!...My ear!!!"

With tightened breath, I looked at Pokey's hand as he drew it away and saw that he was holding a jagged shard of steel shrapnel...not my ear! Pokey looked quizzically amused and chuckled, "What? You want to keep this thing in your ear?!" I felt my ear. It hurt...but it was still fully attached to my head.

As soon as the mcdic bandaged up my worst wounds, we hustled back into the battle. However, the severity of my wounds soon became apparent as my endorphins wore off. The worst shrapnel wound was in my left forearm. A jagged chunk about the size of a nickel had gone all the way to the bone and was throbbing with extreme pain into the evening. Also, a needle-like piece that had entered the front of my throat was creating a slicing pain every time I swallowed.

Darkness fell, and another Medevac helicopter swooped down for a last load of wounded fighters. The throbbing under the bandage wrap on my arm had grown immense, and my head behind my left ear was throbbing too. I knew something was happening inside my head but I didn't know what. Squadmates pushed me toward the nearly loaded, soon-to-depart helicopter. Moments later, I was off into the night sky.

I soon found myself laying on a cot in a base camp MASH tent. Teams of doctors and nurses hustled from cot to cot tending to several dozen wounded men—most of whom were men from our battle. The surgeon dug sixteen pieces of shrapnel out of me, but he said that the x-ray showed a seventeeth piece was deeper in my head, stopping very near my inner ear bones. "We can go after that one," said the surgeon, "but there's a chance that you could end up deaf if we try. If we leave it there, it probably won't give you any problems, and it will eventually just *gristle over*." That was an easy decision for this cowboy…gristle away! So I kept it. Three or four days later, I was back in combat, with stitches that ripped out before the arm wound had a chance to heal. Oh well.

On one of the cots across from me, another GI moaned loudly. He was the driver of the tank that got hit by the rocket, and he now had a crowd of doctors and nurses frantically working on him. Suddenly, the badly wounded GI, whose head and eyes were bandage-wrapped, painfully cried out, "I don't care if my legs will be gone…just tell me if I still have my balls! I want to have children!"

His stunning words hushed everyone in the whole MASH tent! No one spoke…all of us awaited the response from his medical team. After a couple long seconds, the head surgeon replied aloud, "Son, you have a fine set of balls; you'll have your kids some day!" Loud cheers from everyone in the tent erupted as we celebrated a fine set of balls!

My third wound was in another firefight, in a soggy, rain-darkened jungle. Laying behind a tree with bullets socking the tree or sizzling by, I suddenly heard a "thud!" in the soft mud about three feet to my right. It looked like an old can with a bamboo section sticking out of it. I remember thinking, "Is that some kind of stupid joke?!" I stared at it for what felt like long seconds (the actual time was probably less than a single second) before my mind screamed, Grenade!!!"

Pinned down by the intense shooting from my front, I had no safe direction of escape. The only thing I could do was to quickly try to scrunch myself behind the paltry shield of my M-16 rifle and tilt my steel helmet toward the direction of the grenade! In an instant, "BOOOOM!" I felt a big hot blast and the pelting of objects and went numb. I couldn't see a thing because I was engulfed in a cloud of heavy smoke.

When the smoke had drifted away, I felt great relief that I didn't see any dramatic wounds. Then I remembered that I had heard and felt a sharp "clank" against my helmet and a loud "thock" against my rifle. I looked to see a chunk of my M-16 stock was missing, and several other scars on the rifle's plastic. As inadequate of a shield that my rifle was, it blocked some nasty metal from entering the central portion of my body. My steel helmet—whose heavy weight on my head I had often cursed—definitely saved my life!

Later, I discovered that my body had managed to catch some of the grenade's shrapnel. Some small chunks went in and bounced off my breastbone, and others had peppered my right hip. After the battle, I spent some stinging minutes squeezing small pieces of shrapnel up close enough to the surface that I could pick them out with my knife. I didn't need to take up our medic's time; he was busy with worse cases.

Out of the three times I was wounded in combat, the "field-made" grenade's wounds in my hip are the only ones that *still* bother me. Periodically, one or more of those scars will turn bright red and create the most intense, insatiable, fiery itch you can imagine! If it were not for my discovery of hydrocortisone cream, I would not have been able to sleep... *ever!* The torturous itch and lack of sleep surely would have forced me to end my life long ago. Hydrocortisone is one of the most valuable things in my house now.

EVERYDAY MISERY

RAINFORESTS ARE THE MOST DIVERSE PLACES on the planet. The weather is relentless and fierce, and they abound with a plethora of critters that can amaze you, entertain you, feed you (or *eat* you), torment you, and poison you. In short…while there is certainly beauty in Vietnam's rainforests, there is also misery. To delay the trauma of my memories about Vietnam's "critters," I will start with the weather.

The Weather Foe

It was the tropics so Vietnam's winters weren't bitterly cold like in Montana. However, I do remember one time in Vietnam when I shivered hard for most of the night, likely near hypothermia! It was January, and we had been soaked all day and into the night, and were bivouacked in a tight, thick rainforest which afforded us no space for erecting any kind of shelter. We just lay our soaked bodies on the soaked ground in pitch darkness. I'm not sure how cold it got that night, but it likely was in the low 60s! No Montana winter had ever made me shiver so hard and so long. I ended up with a horrible backache from my violent shivering.

Months later, it *really* rained! The Southeast Asia monsoons are rain on steroids! They last about five months and usually peak about the time when the summer heat is the worst. The August rain is quite warm. One of my only nice memories involving monsoons was one afternoon when our company had stopped for lunch. It had been raining all day, but all of a sudden the heavens opened up! You couldn't see more than fifty feet through the incredible downpour. The thought hit us: tear off our fatigues, grab our bars of soap, and then take a *big-time* shower! It was great…because we infantrymen often were dirty from wearing our fatigues and boots twenty-four hours a day. Even at night, sleeping on the ground, we could never take our boots off because we always needed to be instantly and fully combat-ready for an attack. So the cleansing hot monsoon shower felt so good! Ahhhh!

However, the monsoons could go on, and on, and on, and on! There was one miserable period when we were wet day-and-night for fifty-two days! A battalion's four infantry companies usually rotated their time in "the field" for a three-week period; then the longest one out in the field was flown back to guard the artillery base camp for a week where they slept in roofed bunkers that surrounded the base. Being on bunker-line duty, meant that the infantry company got out of the elements and ate hot base camp meals instead of C-rations. However, our fifty-two-day marathon away from our artillery base was because the battalion's A-Company had suffered so many losses that they were too under-manned to leave the bunker line. Thus, we had to stay in the rainy jungles until that company had been fully rebuilt.

A very nasty *misery-on-top-of misery* hit us during those fifty-two days. From having to trek the jungle mountains in soaked boots for so long, our skin had rubbed raw along our boot tops. Ringworm then set in and infected that abraded part of our legs. Ringworm actually has nothing to do with any worms. It's a fungus disease that produces swollen red skin that *itches like hell* at the infection site! We would scratch and scratch the horrible itch all night, which caused infected skin to build up under our fingernails. Then, when mosquitos and leeches feasted on us, we would mindlessly scratch those bites. Soon, ringworm had spread from our fingernails to all those scratched bites…and there were lot of places that needed scratching. Some poor guys had massive patches of ringworm—not just around their boot-tops, but also in their eyelids, crotches, armpits, scalp, their soggy feet…everywhere! Medically, we were a miserable mess! All of that misery while still having to keep sharp concentration on the worse dangers of bullets and shrapnel that were still flying around us!

Our company of soggy, infected infantrymen were so damn miserable that we nearly considered a mutiny if our company commander didn't get us back to the dry bunkers of the base camp! The captain, likewise infected, gathered us all together and sympathized that we all should be in a hospital under normal circumstances! Unfortunately, we had no options until the battered company at our base camp was back up to battle size. The captain, and we, were powerless...and screwed. Medicines that were flown out to us seemed to help only slightly because our company continued to slog it out in a perfect "Ringworm Paradise." I'd guess that some of the worst infected guys may have actually fantasized about getting wounded so they could get flown out of that hell. Unfortunately, some of our beleaguered company actually *did* get wounded or killed...and their torturous ringworm nightmare ended.

Most people think only about battle wounds when they think of how terrible it was to be an infantryman in Vietnam. However, even when not suffering the horrors of combat, infantrymen usually suffered an extreme amount of misery from so many other sources! Our only escape was to numb our brains to what was happening. Our "365-day tour of duty" lasted about a *hundred* mental years.

Vietnam's "Bugs"

Vietnam has so many different species of arthropods that thousands have still never been discovered! Let me start with some of the relatively small animals that people like to call "bugs." This includes insects, giant centipedes, spiders, and scorpions, etc. I will certainly include the world's most common blood suckers, those damn mosquitos in my long "bad guys" list...and those *blood sucking* worms called leeches! There are also a host of other non-bloodsucking crawlies and an insect that I (not so fondly) call "Satan's Pet." But, first...the mosquitos.

The Mosquitos

Always mosquitos everywhere! We all had little bottles of oily repellant that we kept very handy. One particular night with mosquitos, early in my Vietnam stint, really sticks in my mind! We had bivouacked beside some rice paddies; a full moon shined brightly. With the night came biblical hordes and varieties of mosquitos—tiny ones that sounded like gnats, medium ones that sounded like our regular American mosquitos, and huge ones that buzzed like wasps! They filled the night air, which was probably about 95–100 degrees and very humid. Mosquito Paradise.

Out came our bottles of repellant! However, the problem with our mosquito repellant was that it created a Bengay-style warmth effect so that, with the hot night temperature, it was quickly sweat away. It was impossible to keep it sticking for very long, and the swarms then swooped in for the feast on our sweat-washed faces. After a period of futile bug combat that involved wild swatting and "slapping myself silly," I decided that I needed to retreat.

I pulled my poncho liner over my face and body and cowered underneath! Above, on the outer surface of the quilt-like liner, I could actually hear the mosquitos pelting the material as they dove down for a landing, "p...p, p, p...p, p, p, p!" Those pelting sounds combined with the various pitches of different sized mosquitos...all of them loudly demanding, "Come out, you chicken shit, and feed us!" Under the poncho liner, the suffocating temperature quickly rose to what seemed like 400 degrees! Underneath, I would turn into a baked rump roast; outside I would turn into a deflated beach ball. But there were so many of them that they would surely suck me dry!

One thing that I knew for certain, I needed to get sleep in order to be physically and mentally sharp during combat. My only alternative to fighting mosquitos all night, then, was to surrender. Mustering all the superhuman will power that I could, I pulled the poncho liner off and declared myself to be their human feedbag for the night. It was the greatest mind-over-matter stunt of my life. As I lay there, skin-bared, and numbing my mind to the reality of what was happening, I marveled at how many mosquitos could fit on my face at one time. My estimate is that about 50–100 mosquitos continually sucked side-by-side. They filled their bellies tight with fresh blood before leaving and were immediately replaced by 50–100 hungry new ones...coming and going all night long! Literally, tens of thousands of the little bastards were quenched that night by me alone. My bone marrow's blood factories must have been at full throttle all night. But I slept. No mosquito ever called me a "chicken shit" again that night.

The Leeches

Next up, leeches, the other lovely blood sucking bastards. How did we infantrymen survive without regular blood transfusions?! Leeches came in two varieties in my part of Vietnam: large ones that swam like snakes to you when you were in the water, and others that galloped after you, inchworm-like, when you were on land. Leeches are amazing animals! They are so tough that you can boot-stomp on them as hard as you can...and they will just resume their gallop as if nothing happened.

Those land leeches would come after you whether you were momentarily paused on the trail or you were lying on the ground for sleep ...whenever they thought they could gallop fast enough to catch you. But their love for people was a *one-way* love affair! Some of the guys were really freaked out by having a blood-sucking worm on them. I surely didn't like them, but like the mosquito swarms, I soon learned to accept them as just another misery suffered by infantryman.

Leeches are actually pretty amazing little buggers. Once they get on you they move so stealthily that you rarely feel them crawling on you. They have a pain blocker in their saliva which they apply before they slice into you with three razor-sharp jaws. Then they inject an anti-clot chemical to allow your blood to flow freely during their meal. They then suck your blood until they swell up like little balloons...and finally they let go of you to happily digest their fine dinner back on the ground.

Often, the first you knew that you had a leech on you was when you saw a big bloody patch on your fatigues (your blood continues to flow until the leech's anti-clotting chemical is finally washed away in your leaking blood). Sometimes the blood patch was so large that it looked as if you had been shot.

The leeches bothered me the most when I was trying to go to sleep. We infantrymen had to *instantly* be ready for enemy attacks, so we could never sleep in nice zippered tents; we just slept on the ground like animals. When lying still at night, with my skin's senses on high alert, I could sometimes feel them inch-worming on me if they would touch a sensitive nose hair or lip, and their "sneak would be blown."

In the beginning, I would futilely try to tear them in two, but like I described earlier, even stomping boots didn't hurt the leather-tough little buggers! Pitching them into the darkness also proved futile because their acute sense of smell would soon bring them back to me. I finally discovered an effective deterrent! When I caught them crawling on me, I'd bite them in two! Half leeches didn't gallop back to me so well. I guess a man's gotta do what a man's gotta do.

There were two times when the leeches *really* bothered me though! One morning, the last man on guard came around to wake us. I opened my eyes to hundreds of ants scurrying excitedly all over my face and head! I thought, "What fresh hell is this?!!!" The ever-ubiquitous ants didn't usually do that. I sprang to my feet and bent over and commenced briskly brushing them off, sending them flying with my very best curses! Swiping them out of my hair, I noticed that my hair felt tightly *matted!* Once the ants were evicted, I got my comb out to rake it through my hair but the comb met heavy resistance. When I finally got the comb raked through, it was snarled with ripped hairs and big flakes of dried blood! I was pissed! I immediately knew how the blood got there! A damned leech had feasted in my scalp, left, and its anti-clot juice allowed my blood to sponge into my hair where it dried into a crusty mat. With the coming daylight, hungry ants came out and soon found a sleeping head that generously provided them with a yummy jackpot of "dried blood potato chips!" They were considerably more happy with their find than I was!

During another memorable night, I bolted awake with my brain's inner alarm bells clanging away! You know, like when your brain senses that you're about to pee your bed? This time, though, my alarm bells were hollering that I wasn't able to swallow! No matter how hard I tried, I just couldn't swallow! Now, I had never experienced that in my whole life, so I was very concerned. There was moonlight, so I quickly determined where our platoon medic was peacefully sleeping, and I crept over to where he slept. "Doc," I whispered with an anxious tone as I shook his shoulder, "Doc, wake up!"

Woozy, but alarmed that I woke him (medics didn't have to do nightly guard duty), he assumed that enemy soldiers must be near! He sat up and whispered fearfully, "Twiggy! What is it?!"

"Doc, I can't swallow," I answered with obvious angst! Doc tried to clear his head and mentally paged through his brain's files for a medical explanation for *"patient cannot swallow."* But his brain files had no answer. His six-month Medic Training did not include *"patient hasn't been shot through the throat, yet he can't swallow!"*

"Do you have a sore throat?" he drawled with his strong South Carolina accent. "No. I feel fine, but I can't swallow," I replied! "Doc, you gotta help me!" His obvious total lack of an answer showed all over his bewildered face. I became more and more anxious! Was I going to *die* for lack of a swallow, for crying out loud?! Doc couldn't help me. I decided that my only solution was to help myself, so I grabbed his medic bag from beside his head, which is a huge *no-no* because a medics' bag contains heavy drugs like morphine.

"Hey!" the helpless medic protested, "no one is supposed to touch our bag!" He tried to grab his bag back but I gave him a strong shove backward and quickly opened his bag and dumped everything out onto the ground! This was highly inappropriate and illegal, but I had grown very desperate and fearful that my life may be in danger!

The Doc kept trying to stop me but I was too strong for him. I held him away with one hand while my other hand spread out his medical supplies. I had absolutely no idea what I was looking for! All I knew is that maybe—just maybe—a lucky answer might somehow reveal itself!

Suddenly, I spotted something that might possibly help: hydrogen peroxide. Hydrogen peroxide is *really* nasty tasting and it *foams* vigorously when touching a wound or when in your mouth, etc. However, my family had long valued it as a yucky but effective antiseptic gargle when we had a throat ailment...so I snatched opened the bottle, took a big mouth-full, and tipped my head back to gargle deep!

Normally when we gargle, our throats close. But, for a reason that I didn't understand right then, my throat *didn't* close...and hydrogen peroxide plunged down into both my windpipe and esophagus! My body immediately went into a wild convulsive *panic* from the obscene invasion of a nasty chemical into its windpipe and stomach! Hydrogen peroxide foam erupted from my mouth and nostrils, and my stomach immediately went into waves of painful heaves and soon *let fly!!* I turned my head away from the hapless medic's supplies just in time…before vomit and foaming hydrogen peroxide shot forth! The poor medic disgustedly flung himself back out of harm's way. Never before had my stomach and lungs been so completely *pissed* at something that I had given to them!

I braced myself on wobbly hands and knees, and after a minute of vomiting, gagging, foaming, and choking, it finally ended. Gasping and spitting, I was reduced to a shuddering fool of streaming snot and tears, with a puke-y tasting mouth. But I could swallow again! Looking through my tears at the ghastly mess down in front of me, I could see blood and what looked like *"a big squirming blood clot."* What the hell is that?!!! The moonlight soon revealed to my probing eyes what the "squirming clot" was. It was a damn, blood-bloated leech!!!

Oh man, did I ever become a mortal enemy of leeches at that moment! I concluded that the S.O.B. leech must have snuck into my open mouth while I slept, and chose my throat as its place to attach! The exact place of attachment was right across from the lid that is designed to protectively close over the windpipe whenever we swallow anything. As that leech swelled with my blood, it got big enough to keep my lid from closing off either my windpipe or stomach! Earth's gravity then accepted the gargled hydrogen peroxide down into both pipes!

Once the bloody facts finally became understood, our poor medic forgave my illegal intrusion into his bag. He *did* decide to move his sleeping spot away from my disgusting puke pile though.

Other Non-Bloodsucking Crawlies

Vietnam overflowed with a vast array of little critters that biologists love, but which we ground sleepers don't! I saw six-inch yellow scorpions that moved surprisingly fast, and there were also some smaller, *stocky* black scorpions that felt no need to run away at all! I discovered a family of those nasty black devils underneath a rock that I had picked up. They all just turned and faced me with their pinchers up and their deadly stingers aimed over their heads, as if to say "Let us put your name in tomorrow's obituaries, okay?!" They were scary.

Then there were seven-inch long, one-inch wide centipedes! They were fast enough to catch and eat mice! Their sharp venomous jaws told us to leave them the hell alone! We did. Millions of spiders of every size and color were equally abundant because there were so damn many insects for them to eat. Some spiders were big enough to spin a web strong enough to catch flying bats to eat.

One of my men very nearly walked face-first into one of those huge spiders! During the night, the spider had spun its web across the trail along which we all slept. The last man on guard had just woken me and was heading down the trail to wake the other men. I looked upward, from my ground-level perspective, and saw the huge spider on its web silhouetted against the dawning sky—right at the height of his face! I quickly called out, "Stop! Don't move!" He immediately froze absolutely still, and nervously begged, "Where is it?!" "Can't you see it?! Its about one foot in front of your face," I exclaimed! His mind interpreted my emergency tone to mean that I was seeing a booby trap, and his eyes anxiously strained to scan for a trip wire!

Still fearing to move a muscle, he fearfully breathed, "I can't see it!" His brain's "looking-for-a-trip-wire" excluded his eyes from seeing anything except a wire. Plus, the spider's camouflaged body blended in with background foliage so that the only thing he was seeing from his horizontal perspective was just foliage! Finally, half amused but still feeling fearful for him, I said, "Can't you see that spider right in front of your nose?!"

Taking a big sigh of relief that there was no deadly booby trap, he exclaimed, "A spider?!" Rather than fear, his tone suggested great disgust that I'd scared the *shit* out of him over a damn spider! His eyes then readjusted to look for "a damn spider." And then it *came into focus!* "SON OF A BITCH!!!" The GI sprang back like he was shot out of a canon! He turned pasty pale when he saw that he'd been ½ second away from a 3-inch long spider being on his face! He reacted to his intense fright by stepping up and swinging his rifle like a home-run baseball bat! "THOCK!" went the spider! A GI just smacked a spider into the upper left field bleachers! After the GI's heart slowed down, he *thanked* me for scaring the shit out of him...just in time.

Satan's Pet

Last up to bat, an R-Rated run-in that I had with what I refer to as *Satan's Pet!* Sleeping on the ground of a primitive rainforest, we never knew what we'd wake up to: a snake, a tiger, an enemy? Well, one morning I awoke to something *worse!* There was a painful, very alarming sensation coming from my much esteemed, highly prized penis! I immediately opened my fatigue pants with great trepidation to see what the hell was going on! My wide eyes suddenly wanted to go blind! Most of my poor manhood was swollen up to the verge of bursting and was straining downward like it was a lead weight! The base of "Mr. Johnson" was stretched to the diameter of my finger! My eyeballs filled with abject terror, and my mind teleported me out of the Vietnam War Zone and into a worse zone: the *"About To Lose My Penis" Zone!!!"* "Dear Sweet Jesus," I screamed inside my head! "MEDIC!...MEDIIIIIIIIC!!!"

The next thing I remember was standing with my pants down in front of our wide-eyed medic as he checked out the grotesquely frightening sight! Meanwhile, the whole platoon gathered in a horrified circle around us! I was my platoon's unanimous 1968 "Spectacle of The Year" winner! However, I was petrified that I would also end up as the 1968 "Lost Penis of The Year" winner! What happened after that, like most of my terrible combat experiences, is totally repressed. I'd really like to remember but the experience must have been so traumatic that my psyche won't let me remember it. What horrible things could have transpired?!

Did the medic *lance* it with a big needle (Dear God!)...or what?!!!

I do know for sure that my penis did not fall off nor was it amputated. Mr. Johnson is still happily living with me, is normal, and is nicely attached. I never learned what *Son of Satan* bit me that evil night, but I'll admit that the experience dampened my enthusiasm for being in the jungles of Vietnam. I've met a lot of young guys who watch *Rambo* films and wished that they, too, could experience the great adventures of a combat soldier. Hmm, anyone out there still wishing that they were an infantryman in 'Nam? No...I didn't think so.

NIGHT AMBUSH!

WE HAD A SAYING: "THE NIGHT BELONGS TO CHARLIE." (In NATO's phonetic alphabet, C = Charlie and V = Victor. So Viet Cong = VC). The saying referred to the fact that while we GI's moved until the evening, the enemy was typically up moving around during the night.

Because of that, American infantry companies often sent one of their squads out in the evening to set up a hidden site along a trail to ambush the enemy at night. The ambush squad's goal was to kill as many enemies as possible and then quickly get back to the security of their company's encampment. Sometimes, no enemy came by all night. But if the enemy did, it always resulted in ample amounts of adrenaline.

One night ambush has vividly stuck in my mind. My squad was chosen to set up our ambush site a few feet off a very well-used trail that ran through a big, flat, mostly wide-open valley. We could see for about a quarter mile all around us. We tucked ourselves into foliage that lined a small, shallow stream that crossed the trail. Our only real "cover" was having the moon's path behind us so the moon shadow would darken us and the narrow strip of tall bushes behind us. All of the landscape outside of this shadowy strip was spotlighted by the near full moon. From within our dark shadows, it looked nearly like daytime out there.

Ideal ambush sites provided solid cover such as trees, boulders, or earthen berms, plus an out-of-sight escape route if needed. This time, however, our ambush site lacked any of these features. There was no ambush about it. It was strictly an offensive site to quickly wipe out a small band of enemy soldiers before they had any chance to return fire. We also had the advantage of a well-positioned and camouflaged claymore mine, which we had aimed up the trail. Claymore mines were fired remotely, and when detonated, they blasted hundreds of ball bearings in the direction of aim.

Feeling secure enough with our set up, we lay into the reeds beside each other, about a foot apart. As always, we set our M-16's on our laps and had two grenades handy on our ammo belts. The first man in line would hold the claymore detonator "ready" while he stayed awake for our first hour-long guard shift. At the end of his hour, he would give a gentle "two-taps awake" to the leg of next man in line, who would then take the detonator for his own hour-long shift, and so on through the night—one man wide awake on guard while the rest slept.

If an enemy approached, everyone would get a distinct "1-2-3 touch" to get ready for an ambush. Upon a slight signal from the squad leader, the detonation of the claymore mine would initiate the ambush, followed by each GI going for a "kill shot" of his designated enemy soldier. The shooting would continue until it looked like we'd finished them off. Then we'd hustle a retreat back to our company. Usually ambush plans went cleanly but sometimes chaos would ensue on both sides. Our best hope, of course, was that there would be no enemy and no ambush; we draftees wanted to go home alive.

I lay fourth in line from the first man on guard that night, so I oriented myself to my surroundings and then quickly drifted off for my precious sleep. A couple hours later, I felt a "1-2-3 poke" on my leg! That meant, "Enemy!...Everyone ready!" Immediately awake, I looked out onto the brightly moonlit landscape with eyes wide open! My heart sank as I beheld an endless string of NVA soldiers approaching about 400 yards away! And not just riflemen...some were towing large, wheeled, anti-aircraft guns! These NVA were *armed to the hilt!* The trail was going to bring them to within about twenty-five feet from where we lay with no real cover for us except a damn moon shadow! Our eyes were so wide that they nearly burst! Obviously we would not spring the ambush, but we all felt the terror of possibly being spotted! All it would take would be for even *one* of them to peer "just right" into the shadows, because, if it were not for the darkness of the moon shadow, we were in plain sight!

We all slowly readied our M-16's and "froze into stones." In a couple a minutes, the first of the long string of soldiers reached us! "Please, God, keep them looking only ahead!" One after another, hundreds of them marched past us taking what seemed like *forever* to pass! We could see their faces so clearly...spotlighted by the moon and so close that we could hear them breathe! My own breathing was nearly non-existent! I wouldn't have breathed at all if that were an option!

Every enemy soldier toted extremely heavily loaded packs—no doubt with all the ammunition and grenades they could carry. This was a massive troop movement, and we had ringside seats that were way too close! And then they stopped!!!

Our extremely dangerous situation just multiplied (times ten). There stood enemy soldiers as close as only twenty-five feet away! Some of them uncomfortably shifted under their heavy loads, some quietly talked back and forth, some cautiously scanned their surroundings.

And then, an NVA who was among the closest to us looked right in our direction…for about five extremely long seconds! My heart was *pounding* so hard that I literally feared they would hear it. I had the terrifying feeling that he was seeing us! We all intensely studied his body language, his every blink...anything that would indicate that he spotted us there in the dark moon shadow! All M-16's readied for what would be an inevitable bloodbath shootout that would end up with many dead people, including all of us! My racing mind spoke the solemn message, "This is how it's all going to end...get ready to die!"

Thankfully the NVA soldier saw nothing but darkness. The enemy soldiers had been traveling in the direction of a bright moon, which had their pupils too constricted to see our dark shadows! And to our incredible relief, the long enemy column began trekking onward. Heavy packs creaked, chains of machine gun ammo clattered lightly, wheeled anti-aircraft rumbled, and NVA soldiers panted as they passed by a frozen-still band of scared shitless GI's in the shadows! And then they were gone.

We all sucked deep breaths of air! For those terrifying long minutes, we all had been afraid to breathe out of fear that any slight movement might be seen. I probably felt the greatest relief of my lifetime when they had fully passed! Immediately, we got on our radiotelephone and told our company commander the critical information about that enemy force and their map coordinates. A subsequent heated artillery barrage soon followed which lit up the night on the trail where the NVA were headed. It was an immensely intense night for our squad! But, without doubt, a *thousand times* worse for the unsuspecting NVA troops.

THE BATTLE OF KHAM DUC

 located west of
Chu Lai, near the Laotian border. Named after a nearby Vietnamese
village, Kham Duc was built in a narrow valley surrounded by small
jungle-covered hills with high mountain rainforests behind them.
A mile-long airstrip extended NE to SW down the middle. The base was
commanded by the 5th Special Forces Green Berets, and was normally
manned by a few U.S. Air Force air combat controllers, South Vietnam
Army soldiers, Mobile Strike Force troops, civilians, and a platoon of
Australian troops.

In Spring of 1968, U.S. Intelligence reported that a massive ground
attack by 10,000–15,000 enemy troops was imminent. On May 10, that
enemy offensive began about five miles away, just before 3 A.M. The
North Vietnamese Army (NVA) and Viet Cong launched a heavy ground
assault and overran the Ngok Tavak U.S. Marine outpost. Surviving Marines made their way to Kham Duc, which had also come under attack at
about the same time as Ngok Tavak.

The U.S. Army's American Division (AD) responded by launching
"Operation Golden Valley" to reinforce the Kham Duc Special Forces
Camp. My company—the 196th Light Infantry Brigade's 2nd Battalion, 1st
Infantry Regiment (2/1)—was given orders to serve as the reaction force
as soon as the 198th Light Infantry Brigade delivered artillery and ammunition to Kham Duc. After the 198th arrived, they were immediately assigned to "dig in" at the southeast end of the runway near Outpost #1. One

of their platoons dug in to overlook a deep ravine where caves would shield the enemy from any heavy bomb strikes.

Shortly thereafter, at about 3 P.M., my battalion flew in from Chu Lai and immediately began setting up defenses. We were "welcomed" by volleys of enemy mortar shells that rained down on Kham Duc and assigned to an outpost on a nearby hill. When we first got up there, we heard machetes chopping in the jungle below us. A Special Forces sergeant who had accompanied us from the Kham Duc Camp below grinned and shouted, "That's NVA. They're coming to getcha!" We replied, "Yeah...sure!" (as if he thought we were a just bunch of gullible children). "No," he affirmed with a serious face, "They really are...and they're not afraid!" He was right.

Sixty men from the 82nd Artillery and five 105mm howitzers were also brought in. Though under constant mortar and artillery attacks during that time, our Kham Duc forces were still able to strengthen our defenses because there hadn't been any significant enemy ground attacks yet.

After having evening chow, the Marines and Australians were extracted to Da Nang. Allied defenses at Kham Duc were already dangerously thin. But worse, the NVA had occupied much of the higher ground in the surrounding hills where they could fire at allied ground targets and support aircraft with a high level of accuracy! With the departure of the last C-130 flight, the mortar attacks that had occurred every hour or two through the first day finally stopped. The Kham Duc Camp settled down to a suspenseful but uneventful night.

Then, about 9:30 A.M. the next day, May 11th, a UH 1C gunship from the 8th Cavalry was shot down west of Kham Duc by 51-Caliber machine gunfire. This was ominous because it meant the NVA were moving anti-aircraft weapons to the high ground around the camp! NVA ground attacks soon began and were so heavy that thirty B-52 bombers were called in to pound nearby NVA held positions! But the enemy artillery and mortar rounds continued to rain down on Kham Duc and its surrounding outposts, with the NVA and VC eventually surrounding the base. As a consequence, and despite the base being defended by about 1,500 allied soldiers, General Westmoreland ordered Kham Duc to be evacuated. All American and Vietnamese military personnel, as well as their civilian dependents, were to abandon their posts. According to him, with so much nearby high ground the base was too vulnerable and it didn't have "the defensive potential of Khe Sanh."

By 1 A.M. of May 12th, Westmoreland notified the U.S. commanders on the ground in Kham Duc of his decision. However, most army units on the ground were not informed, which led to chaos later when evacuation was underway.

During the predawn hours of May 12th, VC troops continued to increase their pressure on the main compound of the camp. At the same time, the NVA prepared for their main assault by capturing one mountain outpost at a time. The hilltop Outposts #1, #3, and #5 were manned by our 2/1 soldiers, and South Vietnamese soldiers manned Outposts #6 and #7. Some (or all?) outposts had 106mm recoilless rifles and .50 caliber machine guns at their positions. It was Mother's Day, and none of us knew whether we'd ever again be able to celebrate the day with the women who brought us into the world.

Around 4 A.M., our 2/1 soldiers reported that their Outpost #1 above the western side of the camp was being overrun! Fighter bombers were scrambled in an attempt to save it. About 30 minutes later, the defenders of Outpost #7, above the northern end of the camp, reported that their position had been surrounded and was taking heavy fire. They attempted to hold their position by calling on an AC-47 "Spooky" gunship to fire directly into their position in order to stop the massive attack. Spooky's 100 rounds per *second* mini-guns looked like hoses squirting streams of orange fire, with tracers ricocheting off the ground like welding sparks spraying into the air! Nevertheless, Outpost #7 was soon overwhelmed and its defending survivors were forced to retreat down to Kham Duc!

Our soldiers at Outpost #3 came under such heavy attack that there were more NVA coming than could be killed by M-16s and machine guns! The gun battles were at 100% force, and numerous grenades were thrown back and forth. We threw some of our own, plus some of the unexploded enemy grenades, and were forced to radio for Kham Duc's artillery units to fire directly at us in order to keep hordes of NVA from overrunning the outpost! Nevertheless, a few minutes later Outpost #3 was overwhelmed and the survivors were given the dreaded *Escape and*

Evade order—which means, "you're on your own to survive through enemy-held territory!"

It was one half mile or more from the hilltop outposts to the relative safety of main base. NVA were now all around the outposts *and* between us and the base! Being overrun before daylight, parachute flares provided some light, so our escape would have to basically be "running the gauntlet" through the enemy filled dark shadows of jungle! It became "uncertain shoot-outs in the dark" to escape back to Kham Duc! Some soldiers from *both* sides probably escaped being shot simply because the would-be shooter wasn't sure if it was friend or foe running nearby!

Our guys were painfully aware that, if we were lucky enough to get close to the Kham Duc perimeter, *more* luck would surely be needed because our sprinting out of the jungle shadows would be toward perimeter defenders who were mowing down NVA attackers! Bursting from the jungle into the open, everyone screamed, "Americans! Americans" to keep from being mowed down by our own men! One guy was shouting, "Mickey Mantle, Yogi Berra!" The escape was extremely intense!

Eventually, most of the soldiers who manned the dangerous outposts ended up back inside the Kham Duc Camp, where they joined fellow Americans in the trenches shooting NVA attackers who relentlessly charged the perimeter. Unfortunately, however, many of our men who had manned the outposts never made it down.

Near sunrise, the NVA had full control of all seven outposts! That placed U.S. and allied troops inside the base below in an extremely perilous situation! The NVA occupied all of the high ground from which they could fire down on any aircraft that tried to resupply the camp or evacuate anyone! To make our escape even more unlikely, a dense early morning fog moved into Kham Duc valley, and the NVA masses were able to move *very* close to the camp under the cover of the fog!

About an hour before that damn fog lifted, an additional twenty-four B-52 bombers flew in and dropped several hundred *tons* of bombs on NVA positions just south of us. The B-52 strikes told my Charlie Company that huge numbers of NVA had been just over the southern ridge behind our outpost! Around 8:30 A.M., orders came to make an *all-out* effort to evacuate our besieged Special Forces Camp! By 9:30 A.M., the B-52 strikes had clearly failed to stop the North Vietnamese advance, and our southern perimeter was fighting a massive ground assault!

To stop NVA attackers from pouring into Kham Duc, U.S. fighter bombers were called in to strafe the NVA and VC swarms while we on the ground blazed away with our infantry weapons! Our artillery was firing at point blank range to break up the attack! Meanwhile, a U.S. Army UH 1 Huey and an O 2 Skymaster (a small "flying boxcar") were shot down while circling the camp. By the time the southern attack was stopped, the opposite end of the compound also came under heavy fire, and by mid-morning, NVA troops got so close to us perimeter troops, that our fighter jets' bombs and napalm would also kill our own guys!

A U.S. Army CH 47 Chinook helicopter roared in from the northern end to begin the evacuation, but it was eaten up by anti aircraft fire from the captured Outpost #7! The flaming giant helicopter came down hard on the asphalt, but "lucky" crew members scrambled out the back end of their burning craft under the intense cover of machine guns and rockets from its helicopter gunship escorts! The Chinook burst into flames, exploded, and blocked the runway!

Kham Duc soldiers tried to remove the wreckage with a forklift—their only operating vehicle because their bulldozers had been partially disassembled in preparation for airlift out! The forklift caught fire from the burning chopper, so the engineers had to quickly reassemble one of their bulldozers to push the burning Chinook off the runway. NVA troops mortared the bulldozer, but one brave SP5 Don Hostler was able to clear the wreckage and rumble the dozer back and shut it down (God, how *snail-slow* that bulldozer must have felt to its heroic driver)! An Air Force A 1 Skyraider, dropping bombs and napalm on attackers nearby, was shot down as the airstrip was being cleared! Finally, however, troops were able to clear the obstacle that would have prevented any American airplane evacuators/suppliers from using the airfield!

Around 10 A.M., with a clear runway, a C-130 piloted by Lieutenant Colonel Daryl D. Cole touched down on the runway under heavy ground fire that flattened one tire and caused heavy damage to the wing tanks. Immediately, his C-130 was rushed by hysterical Vietnamese civilians from ditches along the runway. Before they could be stopped, they crammed the aircraft so the loadmaster was prevented from unloading the aircraft's vital cargo! Under heavy fire, Cole decided to try to take off, but he had to first weave through an obstacle course of craters and shrapnel on the runway. Finally down the runway, and turned around, he gunned the engines to take-off. Unfortunately, the combined weight of the unloaded cargo and civilians, plus a flat tire and damages sustained during landing, prevented him from gaining enough speed to get airborne! The C-130 was forced to abort takeoff. Only when the plane shut its engines off, did the civilians disembark from the plane and run back to the trenches.

The crew then worked feverishly to remove the flat tire whose flapping slowed the takeoff! They were able to cut the rubber with knives, but had to cut the steel cords with a blowtorch. NVA artillery rounds were zeroing in on his aircraft, so Cole scrambled to take off for the second time. He succeeded to get into the air, but this time his only passengers were the three members of Kham Duc's Air Force Air Combat Control Team whose radio equipment had been destroyed.

All morning long, a fierce battle raged around the airfield with enemy as close as 50 feet! Several airplanes and helicopters had already been shot out of the air! Then an Air Force Forward Air Control plane was shot down but managed to crash land his plane on the side of the runway.

General Westmoreland's C-130 airplane evacuation had been delayed by the burning Chinook blocking the airstrip. Now, all plans were urgently given "The Go!" The first C-130 to land was commanded by Major Bernard Bucher. Bucher landed and loaded his airplane with 150 Vietnamese, mostly civilians. As his airplane lifted off, it flew through the apex of fire from two .50-caliber machine guns, then crashed into a ravine and exploded! All crew and passengers died.

Another C-130 had flown in behind Bucher. Its pilot, Lt. Col. William Boyd, saw Bucher get shot down, so he took off in the *opposite* direction southward and managed to make it to safety despite taking more than 100 hits. However, just after he had taken off, Boyd's C-130 nearly collided mid-air with another C-130 who was coming in from Bucher's landing direction! Apparently, Bucher's landing direction had been assigned to all C-130's! That mid-air collision could have thwarted the Kham Duc evacuation...and hundreds of stranded U.S. troops on the ground would likely have been have been killed by the overwhelming enemy attackers!

The third C-130 was commanded by Lt. Colonel John Delmore. The airplane was hit repeatedly by automatic weapons fire that ripped out the top of the cockpit and shot away the engine controls. Delmore had no choice but to crash land his shot up C-130 and managed to steer it clear of the runway. Meanwhile, U.S. airstrikes were pounding the captured outposts from which enemy guns had shot down Bucher's airplane. Other airstrikes strafed enemy at our perimeter. A fourth C-130 crew got in and out safely and was followed by three others—all under withering ground fire.

While the large C-130 airplanes were landing, the enemy concentrated their fire on them. Army and Marine helicopter pilots took advantage of that distraction and slipped in to make pickups of their own. Within a few minutes, some 500 of the camp's defenders were evacuated.

Many were evacuated before my platoon's turn finally came. Once aboard and airborne, the danger was far from over! Our aircraft was riddled by ground fire...each round sounding like huge hammers pounding on the fuselage! The NVA were fiercely intent on shooting down everyone before they escaped! Thankfully, we did escape.

The declaration by one of Charlie Company's seventeen survivors months earlier—"Ain't none of us going home alive"—went through all of our minds before our bullet-riddled chopper safely landed later! Everyone was painfully aware, however, that the ominous "not going home alive" was unfortunately true for several of our men who never made it out of the Battle of Kham Duc.

By the time that May 10th–12th battle was finally over, the Allied loss tally was as follows:

- Nine U.S. aircraft had been shot down including two C-130 airplanes, two Chinook helicopters, two jet fighters, a Cobra helicopter gunship, a Huey UH-1 helicopter, and an observation plane;
- Hundreds of Americans and our South Vietnamese allies were wounded;

- Over 250 American and Vietnamese allies were killed or missing in action. The combined services reported that the thirty-one U.S. military men reported missing in action at Kham Duc was the highest number of MIA's in any battle in Vietnam. Of those thirty-one MIA's, nineteen were from my 2/1-196th Battalion. Of our own nineteen MIA's, three were rescued within five days, one was captured and imprisoned as a POW until 1973, and fifteen became KIA's (nine bodies recovered, six bodies never recovered).

The crash of Major Bucher's C-130, with all 155 people aboard killed, was the deadliest aircraft crash in aviation history at the time.

Note: Some of the information in this chapter—specifically details related to outposts, loss tallies, names of commanders, etc.—came from research conducted while writing this book coupled with my recollections of Kham Duc.

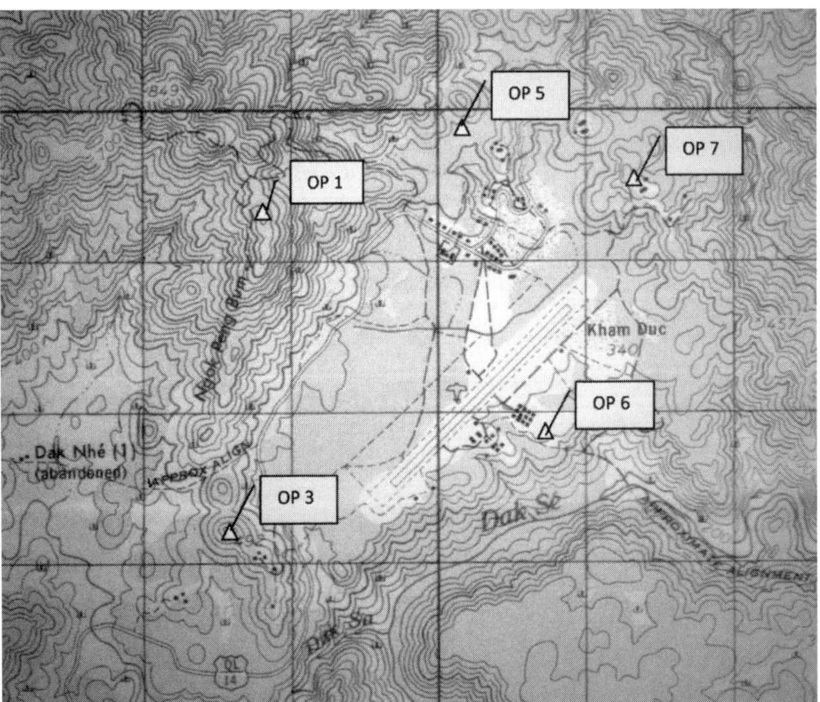

RICE PADDY ADVENTURES

AS INFANTRY COMPANIES MOVE through the swamp-made rice paddy regions, we often use the earthen rice paddy dikes as dry pathways. This mode of travel unfortunately made us vulnerable by putting us out in the open. Though not your basic *safe mode,* it was strategically the quickest way to move from point A to point B. Here are a few memories of our missions in the rice paddy regions.

Adventure #1

We often came under sniper attack while moving along these dikes. The first one of these sniper attacks that I remember happened around the first week that I was in Vietnam. At the time, I was assigned to be the RTO (radiotelephone operator) of our platoon leader. Being an RTO is *not* a fun job! It meant carrying a heavy communications radio in addition to the already heavy infantryman's backpack. Plus, the radio's long antenna sticking up made you a prime target for the enemy!

On that particular day, I was trudging along behind my platoon leader as our company moved single-file up the middle dike of a narrow two-paddy-wide valley. Suddenly, heavy sniper fire erupted from the jungle hillsides that bordered the sides of the paddy! With bullets splashing all around us, everyone took off running toward the wooded cover at the base of the snipers' hillside. Unfortunately, the lieutenant and I were halfway between the perpendicular *side-to-side* dikes, so the fastest route to reach tree cover was directly through the eighteen-inch deep rice paddy!

Running through water with a gooey bottom is difficult under *any* circumstances but, with my heavy pack plus the radio *and* pneumonia-weakened legs, I struggled to keep up with the rest of the platoon. The next thing I knew, I stumbled and plunged headfirst into the brown rice paddy water, with my upper body and head weighted underwater by the twenty-five pound radio! I clearly remember my abject panic and terror as I realized that I was probably the only non-running target in the paddy; I was a flashing-red sitting duck! You can probably imagine the underwater sound of bullets smacking the water and zipping lines of bubbles down into the mud around me! However many seconds that I desperately floundered under water, it felt like forever...waiting for a bullet! My miraculous escape is a total blur though! I somehow eluded likely death, but the traumatic details of my harrowing escape got crammed into my deep repression chamber.

Adventure #2

Another sniper attack happened one morning when an unusually large infantryman recruit joined our company. About 6′ 4″ and 230 pounds, he was quickly placed in the rifle sights of a lurking sniper who picked him out as the easiest target. "Pow!" Down went the big guy a few yards in front of me! We quickly dragged him to cover. Though not fatally wounded, he was hit by the sniper's bullet square in his right butt cheek. After being given morphine and bandaged up, he expressed only elation that he only had to spend a lousy three hours as an infantryman in Vietnam! Still sporting his bright white untanned skin, he would soon be on his way home to the safety of American soil. With a bullet yet to be dug out of his ass cheek, he still felt like a lucky man. We kinda understood.

Adventure #3

One late evening near dark, my company was trekking up the dike of a wide rice paddy. At *that* time, my assigned weapon was the M-79 Grenade Launcher, which is a short but heavy shot gun-like weapon that shot a fat 40mm grenade which exploded on contact.

I was fourth in line behind the point man, when suddenly I heard him yell, "Dung lai!" (that's Vietnamese for "Halt!"). I looked up to see an armed Viet Cong sprinting across a paddy dike toward the left tree-line about 100 yards ahead, with no intention of halting! The guys in front of me opened up with their M-16's, and red *tracer rounds* zinged past the racing enemy soldier!

The fleeing Viet Cong managed to evade the shower of bullets and disappeared into the safe darkness of the tree line. Instead of continuing on to safety, however, he slipped back to the dark edge of the vegetation to return a parting volley of his own. From *my* vantage point, I was able to spot his silhouette sneak back and raise his rifle. I quickly aimed my M-79 and fired!

The result was a dramatic combat spectacle! The Cong's dark silhouette was suddenly lit up by a bright flash with red-orange sparks shooting out in all directions! I had made a direct hit on the enemy soldier's chest! It would be inhumane to describe the gory aftermath, but our whole platoon was soon able to view the savage power of an M-79 round when it makes a direct hit!

Adventure #4

This rice patty memory nearly had *me* as the victim. As was typical, my platoon was moving uncovered up the middle of a wide rice paddy system one late afternoon. Suddenly, several snipers opened up on us from their cover on one of the heavily wooded hillsides that rose up from each side of the paddy. This time, however, a bushy hedgerow extended lengthwise up the middle of the paddies. A hail of bullets was coming from the hillside on our right, and the hedgerow was our nearest cover—albeit only *visual* cover. The hedgerow bushes were too thin to actually stop any bullet, but at least they were thick enough that the snipers couldn't see us behind them. Snipers continued firing into our hedgerow hoping that some lucky bullets would find us.

The order was given for my platoon to engage the snipers while our company's other platoons maneuvered on the enemy. This order meant that we had to regularly expose ourselves from behind *crappy* cover to shoot. So, we would stand up every few seconds to fire a couple of quick rounds, then duck back down and quickly shift our hiding position. Each time invited a volley of lead!

During this "rise-fire-duck" maneuver, I had just popped up...but before I could fire a single shot, there was a loud buzz accompanied by a "flick" on the bottom of my left ear lobe and cheek! A sniper bullet had just touched the left side of my face!!! I had inadvertently risen into wild bullet! The bullet had apparently clipped a branch somewhere between the sniper and me, throwing the bullet into an erratic tumble that caused the bullet to buzz past like a very loud bee!

A *very* near miss! My body attempted to duck faster than was humanly possible! Once I had safely ducked and shifted, however, something strange happened that hardened infantrymen might understand: wide eyed, I grinned broadly! I looked around me, and my squadmate beside me was grinning too! *"Close one,"* he said.

That strange reaction to a potential fatal moment was an anomaly, of course. Whenever bullets *connected,* there were no grins. However, our "rice paddy grins" did demonstrate that combat is surely the most intense adrenaline rush in the world! That time, I merely "got buzzed!"

That said, in my opinion, if folks want intense excitement, I would strongly suggest a wild roller coaster ride...without bullets.

Adventure #5

This adventure didn't involve fighting, but it was interesting. My company was coming down a remote, dried up rice paddy one sunny morning. Near the upper end of the paddy system, I looked about twenty-five yards to my right and saw a peculiar sight. It was the body of a dead Vietnamese man…and his skin was a hard-looking, *shiny black* instead of the gray colors of decomposition. Every strand of muscle showed clearly. The man had died in a sitting position against the dry rice paddy's earthen dike—almost like he was taking a nap. It looked surreal because he was such a perfectly preserved mummy…almost an attractive, shiny, obsidian black figure!

I must have been in Vietnam for a while because I felt zero shock or sorrow—only interest. It's pretty strange how the mind can switch off emotions at times. A mere year earlier in Montana, if I had come across a dead body in the countryside it would have been a very big event in my life. I would have been aghast. But there I was, dispassionate about a poor dead man. Who was he? A farmer whose sad family was home wondering where he was? A Viet Cong who was mortally wounded by a GI? Or maybe one of America's Vietnamese *allies* who was shot by a Cong or NVA foe? Did his family and friends ever find him to give him a decent burial? Hmm. In America, we often take life totally for granted.

But there in Vietnam, life was fragile. Very fragile.

SUICIDE AMBUSH

IN OUR INFANTRY COMPANY, squad-sized ambush missions were frequently ordered. Upon getting this order, we always felt apprehension and full of adrenaline. Sometime between dusk and dark, we (usually seven to ten guys) would leave our company's bivouac camp, never knowing exactly what was in store for us. The ambush mission could just as easily have resulted in no encounter...or a night of death.

One particular ambush mission is especially memorable for me. Its intensity caused heavy repression and fragments of mysterious, free-floating images in my mind for decades. Through personal therapy with a very skilled veterans' counselor in 2003, I was able to uncover some of the repressions of that ambush and assemble some of my mystery images into a sensible picture.

On this particular ambush mission, I was one of seven members of our depleted squad who were on our way to an assigned ambush site at dusk. We had gone about a mile from our company's bivouac site, traveling along a trail that ran up the middle of a wide river's 200 foot-wide flood plain.

A thick jungle that extended into high rain-forest mountains grew along on the left side of the flood plain. The plain was grassy with a scattering of three- to four-foot high bushes...practically open. At the moment, our trail had curved to within about fifteen feet of the river to avoid a dense thicket that grew along a streambed that extended in front of us to the river on our right.

We arrived at the dry streambed, which had an eight-foot-deep, thirty-foot-wide washout that had been created by monsoon rains. We had just dipped down into the washout and were heading toward its far bank. The point man had reached the top edge of the bank when, suddenly, he spotted enemy NVA soldiers ahead!

Ducking back into the cover of the streambed, we all peered out at about eighty heavily armed NVA soldiers rounding a left bend of the river. They were randomly spread out on our flood plain about 600 yards ahead...and traveling directly toward us! Their lack of quick movements indicated that they had not seen *us* yet. As we watched, more soldiers continued to come into view from around the bend. Many more!

Immediately we radioed everything about our situation to our platoon leader, who happened to be a young and very "green" lieutenant. We expected that his response would be to ask for the enemy's coordinates and, as is typical, call for an artillery barrage upon the unprotected mass of enemy soldiers. Then we would retreat back to our company under the cover of that artillery.

Instead, to our abject shock and horror, he ordered the seven of us to hold our position and to ambush them! Apparently, the lieutenant wanted us to wait until the enemy was right on top of us and then open fire to kill a large number of them...a big fat "body count" scored for his command! By the time the lieutenant finished his order, at least 150 NVA had come into view, with still more coming behind them out of sight around the bend. We looked at each other in disbelief!

Thinking that the Lieutenant must have missed our description that there was nothing behind us except a long stretch of open plain (no cover), we repeated our situation and updated the enemy number to more than 150 soldiers. A terse reply came back that he *did understand,* was ordering an ambush, and questioned whether we "had a problem carrying out his order!"

Our squad had been anxiously crowded around our field radio to hear the lieutenant's orders, which—once confirmed—were greeted with highly agitated curses: "Bullshit!" "Fuck you man!" and "To hell with that shit!!!" We were being given a *suicide mission!*

An artillery barrage, too, would produce a large "body count"—without sacrificing our lives! We all quickly agreed that there was no way that we were going to carry out this order! Just as we were about to radio our proclamation of defiance, which would result in our being busted to the rank of buck private and being court-martialed, we looked up and saw that the NVA were now only about 300 yards away. However, they had stopped traveling toward us! Instead, they had turned en masse and were heading to our left into the thick jungle tree line!

Great surprise, relief, and wide smiles filled our faces! It seemed too good to be true but, we reasoned, the enemy was perhaps heading into the jungle to bivouac for the night! The horrible predicament of our suicide order would be avoided! Man! It seemed like we were being given a holy intervention by God Himself!

Trying not to sound like a giddy bunch of schoolboys, we quickly radioed the new situation back to camp. The Lieutenant modified his orders; but instead of "return to camp," his new order was to hold our position, and to execute his ambush order if the enemy re-emerged from the tree line.

"That was good enough for now," we all thought. It seemed unlikely that the enemy would come back out of the forest once they had gone in. Apprehensively, we took up ambush positions in the streambed, and peering out into the late evening landscape in front of us, we all prayed. Our best hope was that the enemy's intention was to continue on through the jungle, and on into to the mountains that arose nearby. Our draftee band of seven GI's wanted no part of a gung-ho band of 200 or more NVA soldiers *nor* did we want to face a life-wrecking court-martial!

Darkness was nearly upon us as we tensely waited. A few very long minutes passed and it looked like our prayers had been answered. Unbeknownst to us, however, our streambed did not extend directly from the river beside us to the mountains. The streambed actually ran through that jungle tree line into which the NVA had disappeared, and then curved right down to where we were! To our great misfortune, the NVA soldiers had discovered the same dry riverbed where we quietly "laid in wait" and then they chose it as their new path!

So there we were, all eyes directed forward to the plain and tree line ahead, tensely waiting for the enemy to NOT emerge from the jungle. Suddenly, a slight sound to our left made us glance up the streambed. To our stark horror, the streambed (which *had* represented our only cover before) was suddenly full of NVA soldiers! Amazingly, they *still* had not seen us lying motionless in our ambush positions, but now they had walked right up on us…to within thirty feet away! Holy shit!!!

With absolutely no time to think, we whirled and started blazing away! Both we and the NVA were in full panic! Since we had seen them first, however, the advantage was still on our side—at least for a few more seconds! Gunned-down NVA were dropping all over the streambed! There were more than we could shoot even at close range! Those who hadn't yet been shot were diving for cover into the thick vegetation that walled the sides of the streambed.

Instinctively knowing that the enemy was in momentary chaos, and that we had just fleeting seconds to escape, the squad leader hissed a quiet "Psst!" to us, and motioned a quick but quiet retreat! We bolted and ran for our lives in the direction of our company camp! We emptied our belts of grenades as we ran, heaving them back into the streambed where the enemy still lay hiding. That strategy bought us valuable seconds—however many it took the enemy to recover—but extra (and welcomed) seconds nonetheless.

We had sprinted for about 150 yards across that damned open flood plain before the air began to fill with bullet lead! We were without any cover for what seemed like forever! We zigzagged to create more difficult targets, but that didn't gain us as much distance as running in a bee line and *distance* was our best friend! It seemed impossible to not get shot because there was such intense AK-47 and machine-gun fire streaming all around us with terrifying hisses! Throughout our dash, I excruciatingly waited for the imminent "THUMP" on our backs!

My memory is that we all somehow escaped alive and unwounded! However, I have no memory of our finally getting back inside our company's encampment. My not remembering our *likely joyous* return both confounds me and concerns me. Could my lack of memory mean that tragic "thumps" *did* occur during our harrowing dash? (I believe that

95 percent of my experiences in Vietnam have been scrubbed from my memory—both a blessing and a frustration)!

I know that at least one very important part of that ambush scene had *indeed* been repressed until it was revealed during a counseling session with my VA counselor in Great Falls in 2002. Here is the story of that amazing revelation.

The Old Man in the Streambed

Let me preface this revelation with a couple of facts to give perspective to the experience. In the years that followed my return from Vietnam, some of my combat images would drift in and out of my memory. Many of these images were no more than mere "snapshot photos" of faces or scenes...providing me with no before-or-after context. These "free-floating still-shots" would appear in my mind at random times. I was always frustrated because these unattached images were mysterious visitors who would never *identify* themselves! Why did I keep seeing them? What significance did they have? Logic told me that they must be important or they wouldn't keep haunting me—even decades after Vietnam!

One such image was the face of an old peasant man wearing the traditional black clothing and conical grass-woven hat that most Vietnamese peasants wore. This old man's face haunted me often! His deeply lined old face always appeared to be looking at me with such intensity that his eyes seemed to bore right to the center of my soul! His expression was pained and seemed to desperately plead for my attention! Every time his face would appear in front of me I would always wonder, "Who *are* you?!" "Why do you keep coming to visit me decades after I was in your country?!"

The mysterious old man finally "identified himself" during my 2002 Great Falls counseling session. After months of counseling, I had developed a close and trusting therapeutic relationship with the counselor, Tony Rizzo. I had recounted this ambush story to friends and relatives several times for years, and now I was again recounting the "suicide ambush" story to Tony. However, in telling it to Tony, something very dramatic happened! When I got to the part in which my squad looked up and saw the enemy only a few feet from us—and we started blazing away in panic—that old man's face suddenly appeared in the scene!

At first, I felt much surprise and confusion that this old man's face was present in the battle scene that I was describing. Then, to my stunned shock, his image slowly inserted itself into the face of the nearest "NVA soldier" in that the streambed!!! In reality, that old man was actually leading them, and it was *he* who was the nearest man to me! The NVA had probably forcefully "recruited" the old man on their way and made him come along to tote two large baskets of rice on his old shoulders… making him walk in front of them as a human shield/point man.

I was horrified as the full reality of that violent evening in Vietnam unfolded! In a horrible misfortune of circumstances, my squad had earlier been watching a large force of NVA soldiers travel right toward us; we knew that we would all be killed if we engaged them. Our minds were highly charged! Consequently, when we looked up and saw our streambed full of NVA soldiers, our minds saw *nothing* but soldiers! The sudden extreme danger and close proximity of the NVA troops put us in a full panic mode, and our survival depended on an instantaneous and deadly response!

In the first *lightning strike second,* my mind "put an NVA uniform on the old man" and then immediately blocked out that I was shooting a civilian to death! The imminent threat of the *many* NVA with the old man would not let me pause for even one damn split-second to consider the horrible reality! However, my "see all" subconscious mind recorded every microsecond! Once the old man "had finally identified himself" to me in Tony's counseling office, my subconscious mind found the courage to "rewind the tape" and then play it forward in the following excruciating detail:

When the first of my rapid-fire bullets hit the poor old man in the chest, his eyes first widened in extreme shock! As I fired another quick shot or two, his expression quickly flashed to a horrified awareness of the mortal damage! Immediately his eyes very intently pled with me, "No! No! I'm just an old man!" Finally his eyes, still locked onto mine, turned to deep sadness before he crumpled...he knew that he was being shot to death.

Tears filled my eyes in the counselor's office as my conscious mind saw every painful detail in the incredible *slow-motion replay* that the human brain can produce in very extraordinarily dangerous events. For decades, my mind had protected me from that shameful part of the ambush! During my time in Vietnam, I had always maintained a sincere respect and reverence for the civilians—even protecting them at great risk to myself at times! The sudden knowledge that I had killed one of those civilians—a helpless old farmer—was a soul-slashing pain for me!

Shame and horror immediately competed for the top rung in my mind when the old man revealed his identity. It was a bitter reality for me to gain! My accepting that reality and *forgiving* myself became the counseling focus for the remainder of that session and other sessions to come.

After much work, I managed to come to terms with what happened. I know in my heart that the departed spirit of the old man understands this too and fully forgives me. My feelings for him are very reverent and tender. I'm now clear that the old man was one of the war's many innocent civilian casualties...civilians whom I had always *protected!*

In reality, both the old man and I were victims of the dreadful circumstances that occur in the chaos of war. The old man, whom I had met for only one eternally long second, died, and I lived. He was a peaceful old farmer who should have lived...I was a combatant who should have died by NVA bullets. But war chooses no favorites; it only chooses death. War is not glory; it is only hell.

THE SHITTIEST COMBAT MISSION

CHARLIE COMPANY HAD MANY TOUGH and shitty missions in Vietnam. This is the story of one of the most memorable of those.

This mission was in a high mountain rain forest region in the northern part of South Vietnam. My company was in hot pursuit of a North Vietnamese infantry company that we had been chasing through the dense jungles. Occasionally, we would catch them, and there would be a firefight until they broke away. We would then continue after them until we caught them again and had another battle. This chase/battle continued for several days. It was a battle of attrition and we were continually coming out on top. It seemed like we would eventually finish them off.

At one point in our pursuit, the NVA troops temporarily gave us the slip by leaving the main trail and heading up a rocky streambed that crossed the trail along the way. A half-day later we figured out what they had done, backtracked, and headed up the stream.

This stream was warm as bath water, like all streams in Vietnam were, but it was a clear, pristine stream, tumbling down through the beautiful Asian rainforest. Infantrymen filled their canteens from such clear streams...and then (for purification purposes) made that water taste really, really bad by adding disinfectant iodine tablets to the water. As a result, our drinking water usually tasted like chlorinated laundry water. Yechh! Sometimes, however, when we were around a stream as pristine as this one, we cheated and didn't use the iodine tablets. Oh, how nice it

was to drink pure water once in a while! And so we decided to cheat this time; a reasonable risk, we thought.

A reasonable risk...until the moment in our upstream pursuit when we found, to our horror, a slaughtered water buffalo in the middle of the stream! Warm water had been flowing into the animal's guts, and then downstream into our canteens...and into our unsuspecting intestines!

Many thoughts went through our heads upon seeing this—none of them good! The NVA had obviously killed and hacked open one of their large pack animals in order to disgustingly sabotage our pursuit! It was a simple *biological warfare weapon* for stopping us!

In the previous hour, several of our guys had noted ominous rumbles in their guts. Upon seeing the grotesque sight of this rotting animal in our drinking water, *all* of us started to feel the same rumbling. We knew we were screwed; we just didn't know how *badly* we were screwed yet.

Soon, all of us were experiencing horrible cramps. Climbing any farther up the steep streambed or going back down just wasn't going to happen with us all painfully doubled over with cramps. Our company commander knew that our pursuit had ended, so he ordered us to set up camp.

One of a company commander's tasks is to plan strategic routes on his topographical map. This includes planning a decent nightly campsite for his company. It *normally* works that way...an infantry company ended its daily trek at a reasonably comfortable, defensible bivouac site. However, our current *emergency* campsite was not topographically good at all! We were stuck high on a very steep, large-bouldered mountain streambed, the sides of which were walls of very *dense* thickets of rain forest jungle. Moving even two feet into that jungle was very tough, so setting up any *decent* camp in the forest would be impossible! However, we had no other alternative but to try; everyone was excruciatingly cramped up...and squirting!

The only way we would create our sleeping place for the night was to cut narrow paths into the thick jungle with our machetes, then chop out small nooks where we could lie down. This was hard work under any circumstance...but by now all of us were exploding with severe dysentery!

Our daylight was disappearing. Our "repeating scenario" was basically: "chop, chop, chop then quickly drop our pants and crap," "chop, chop, chop then quickly drop our pants and crap," *ad nauseum* (pun intended!). Our chore was nothing short of miserable, *miserable,* misery!

Painful dysentery, steep slope, and disappearing daylight eliminated any luxury of creating a spacious camp. Everyone wanted to swing that damn machete as *little* as possible, thus each man chopped a very short path to his little sleeping nook—only two to three feet away from the next man's. We were practically going to be sleeping on top of each other, but we were so sick and weak that the only thing on our minds was finishing our meager nook and getting off our feet!

Most guys then rummaged around in their packs to find something that sounded good to eat. Our bodies needed energy to replace everything that was coming out of our back ends. Our stomachs demanded food, so we ate! Soon after, our intestines *cursed* our stomachs; "You STUPID JERKS!" they screamed in dissent at the food we were attempting to digest. Our new "repeating scenario" then became "chomp, chomp, crap, crap...chomp, chomp, crap, crap." "Oh, *Dear God,*" our rear ends cried, "Make it stop!" (This is my anthropomorphic interpretation of the *actual* voices that were coming out of all parts of bodies, backsides included!).

One hundred men, crammed into an intimately tight space, all suffering from severe dysentery, was surely about as bad as it could get! At least I thought that was the case! No, it got worse. Dark clouds covered the sky and rain fell as the night began, making it so dark that we couldn't see our hands in front of our faces!

Vietnam infantrymen know all too well the realities of spending the night in pitch-dark rain. You can't see the enemy, but what the hell, they can't see you either. In that total darkness you feel reasonably safe. However, on *this* particular night, *none* of us felt safe! We were blasted by constant "incoming rounds"...not from bullets, grenades, or mortars, but from blasts of diarrhea! Lots of it! From every direction! From every butthole! All night long!

Despite our extreme fatigue, sleep was nearly impossible! We would just doze off, only to be awakened by severe cramps and an urgent call to immediately get up and squirt. But do it *where?!* Well, anywhere *except* into your own little nook of course. But, in pitch darkness on a steep, wet slope, we couldn't walk anywhere (flashlights could invite enemy grenades…a big no-no)! So, everyone spent the night trying to sleep, while at the same time needing to stay alert to try to hear any other GI getting up near them! Thus, the night passed with the steady sound of rain constantly interrupted by the sound of "SPPPLLTTT!"…immediately followed by someone's "Hey, you son of a bitch!" Then, "Sorry man, I can't see!!!" And, minutes later, "SPPPLTTT! BLA-A-A-T-T-T!" Then, very angry cursing, "God damn it! I'm *shooting* the next asshole who shits on me!!!" But what could we do? The amoebas in our intestines were in full command of the situation, er…"*shit*-uation."

After what seemed *forever*, the first dim light of day finally came! Our only thought: "Get us the *hell* out of here!" We were all so sick, weak, and still cramping with horrible diarrhea, that we *almost* didn't care about what the light of morning revealed! However, as one might expect, what it revealed was a scene not for weak stomachs. We were all covered with yellowish-brown diarrhea! Our jungle fatigues were soaked, and our hair was a gooey, sticky mess! And, although the parts of our brains that sense odors had gone totally *numb* hours earlier, we reeked!!

I looked down at the place where I had been "sleeping," a nice hollow in the ground, which I had cleverly created the evening before by rolling a log away. My *comfy little cradle* had become a trough of a nasty yellowish soup of rainwater and diarrhea—*ear-hole* deep! The bottom half of my body had been submerged in that all night long. That disgusting thought would have spoiled my breakfast appetite if I *had* any. We all looked at each other in disgust! We didn't know whether to laugh or to cry. Mostly we laughed—in between retching and more squirting. Our only consolation was that we had little left to squirt.

The company commander told us that he had radioed Headquarters the night before to describe our bad situation. Battalion HQ promised to send helicopters with medicine, clean water, and clean clothes! Thank God! The only problem was that we were still on very steep terrain with very tall trees—impossible for a helicopter to land. Therefore, we would have to painfully descend back down the bouldered streambed and then trek several more miles down to the nearest flat, open ground where a huge Chinook helicopter could land. Painful dysentery or no painful dysentery, that was our only solution. Doubled over with wicked gut cramps, we were sure that the trek out of the mountains would not be fun! But we were infantrymen...and infantrymen aren't supposed to have fun!

By the time that we were finally out of the mountains and out of their clouds, the shining sun had dried our wet fatigues. Large yellowish-brown patches of dried diarrhea created a devil's artwork of interesting designs all over our fatigues (clever art, Satan)! When we finally reached our flat, open rendezvous area, two helicopters soon arrived. A big Chinook was toting a heavy water tank that hung from a cable underneath it. The other helicopter was a smaller Huey that was toting medicine and a large net filled with enough clean clothes for the whole company. I'll never forget the horrified and absolutely disgusted looks on the faces of the helicopter crew as they landed as our mob of shit-covered infantrymen surrounded their helicopter and rummaged through the pile of clean fatigues to find tops and bottoms that fit. The insensitive flight crew spent the entire time gagging, pinching their nostrils, and shouting insults and curses!

I'm sure it was a sight to behold: a hundred naked guys with sticky, gooey hair all digging through the big pile of clothes. Unfortunately for the gagging crew, their orders were to stay until we had gotten our clean fatigues and had reloaded our dirty shit-covered fatigues back into their net. Then, they were supposed to transport the net full of soiled fatigues back to the base camp laundry. The crew gagged the whole time. We just couldn't muster up any pity for them, sitting in their clean helicopter, wearing their clean pressed uniforms. Poor babies! I'm sure that the helicopter crew complained for the rest of their lives about what "*tough* duty" they had to suffer through that day. Yeah...suffering is a *relative* term, boys.

Meanwhile, we gulped some "anti-amoebic dysentery, butt plug" pills and immediately headed over to the nearby stream with our bars of soap and clean spairs of fatigues! Having laid our precious clean clothes on the bank, we began de-shitting ourselves in the stream's warm pools!

Behind us was the sound of helicopters roaring away at full throttle! Seconds later, as we joyfully shampooed shit out of our hair and scrubbed our bodies in the stream, we watched the helicopters rising near the crest of the jungle mountain ridge. The helicopter that was towing the net full of diarrhea-soaked clothes suddenly dropped their cargo into the jungle below them! Did their net cable accidentally slip?

Naaaah, no accident. We understood.

THE ENDLESS GREEN DEEP

HAVING GROWN UP AS A LANDLUBBER ALL MY LIFE, I often rued that my infantry company was never given a mission down by the ocean. However, I did manage to get to the ocean beach *without* my infantry company. That one time was an extremely unforgettable one.

Soon I was walking barefoot on the warm white sands of a huge GI-crowded beach! I was exhilarated because it felt like an unexpected, awesome vacation from combat! "Next best thing to Hawaii," I thought! I had never learned how to swim, but my fears of the ocean were allayed when I learned that it was only five feet deep 100 yards from shore at this beach! Wow, I could get out there and safely enjoy the warm waters of the South China Sea!

My buddy showed me how to body surf. Simply wade out to chest-deep water, wait for a wave to come, leap upward and let the wave ride me to the shore. Wow, it was incredible fun to be able to totally enjoy playing in the ocean for the first time in my life! And, dear God, how my bleeding combat spirit needed to have fun!

After several hours of body surfing wave after glorious wave, I had finally exhausted myself. I stood up in about three feet of water and scanned the beach for where I had laid my towel. "Oh, *there* it is, about 40 yards up the shore to my right." I decided to wade directly toward my towel...*angling* into the shore. As I waded nearer, I noticed that the outgoing water was getting swifter even as the water grew shallower. "Hmm, curious," I thought to myself. I plodded onward until the knee-deep water was so swift that I needed to dig my toes into the sandy bottom to stay standing. Suddenly, the swiftness of the current got so strong that it vacuumed all the sand out from under my straining feet, and down I went. Immediately it was like I was in a giant toilet that just got flushed, and I felt myself tumbling underwater away from shore!

Finally flailing my way to the surface, I was shocked beyond shock to find that I was about 400 yards from shore! My heart sank to see people *looking so small* in the distance! Again I sank beneath the surface. My toes desperately reached downward for a sandy bottom; I found nothing but water...and I can't swim! I had heard of the term "riptide" before, but I really didn't know what riptides were. Now, in only a few seconds, one had jet-boated me to the chasm of death!

My struggling arms got my face above water for another gasp of air, but the moment was so brief that I managed only a very quick "Help!" Underwater again and desperately exhausted, I saw nothing but green water and a shimmering ball of sun in the direction that I knew was up.

My leaden arms and legs barely got me up for one last gulp of air before water poured into my nostrils and I sank again. Exhausted even before the riptide flushed me out to sea, I was finally drained of every last drop of strength. And I sank. Down into an *alien* world of light green that seemed to go on forever, there was nothing left but the numbing reality that I was about to be a dead person.

It was a profound aloneness. Yet I felt a helpless calm as I drifted downward into the endless green abyss. I felt like a spectator to my own death. For months I had an ever-present feeling that one of the hundreds of bullets that were fired at me might end my life. But now, it seemed so surreal; *drowning* would be my end! As I stared down at the green nothingness into which I was disappearing, my mind filled with thoughts of my family back home, especially my Mom and Dad! I felt like I was about to deliver my ultimate failure as a son. I prayed to them with the last seconds of my life, "Please forgive me for not coming home."

Suddenly...I felt a slap on the top of my head and a firm pulling of my hair, followed by a sensation of being pulled upward. I was then able to make out a paddling arm of someone above me, and in seconds, a young guy was hauling me onto a surfboard and was pounding my back! My stunned mind's first thought as I choked out water was that someone appeared out of nowhere to save my life! My second thought was of the bizarreness of finding myself on a surfboard in Vietnam! As an infantry grunt who dwelled mostly in mountain jungles, a *surfboard* was the very *last* place where I expected to find myself during a war! But, oh how good that surfboard felt to my limp, near-drowned body!

I remember only a little more of that day's close brush with death: the young hero was a California surfer who was stationed at the Chu Lai military base, and he'd had his surfboard shipped over to him. He had been relaxing on the beach when he heard guys yelling that someone was drowning way out there! Very familiar with that beach, he grabbed his surfboard and plunged into the riptide, giving him added speed for paddling out to where guys had seen me go under. He later said that he made several passes back and forth without seeing anything to give him hope. Finally, he spotted my dark hair far below the surface, and dove!

Being drafted and sent to Vietnam was every young American man's greatest fear back then, but I feel deep gratitude that one "beach bum" *also* got drafted in 1968. My un-named California friend, I hope that I thanked you enough that day, but here's another thank you from the deepest part of my heart! Because of you, over a thousand students, years later, sat in a Montana classroom of a very passionately driven and caring science teacher. Because of you, I have two beautiful daughters who have dedicated their lives to helping other people in our world. Because of you, my family saw me return home from Vietnam only to become the butt of one of their funniest Scrabble stories.

Yeah, well n*o thanks* for that *last* part.

THE MOMENT OF DEATH

MANY THINGS ARE EXPERIENCED BY THE SOULS who go through heavy combat. There are many intensely exciting things, tragic things, and terrifying things...some so terrifying that the mind *immediately* erases them from consciousness. I served in Vietnam from the very start of the bloody "Tet Offensive" and was assigned to Company C of The 196th Light Infantry Brigade's 2nd Battalion of the 1st Infantry Regiment (C 2/1, 196th). Ten months before my arrival, my Charlie Company had been reduced to only a fraction of the normal one-hundred twenty men. Later, two to three weeks before I joined that company, it was decimated again to a mere seventeen hardened survivors of another horrible attack in which "Charlie" was completely overwhelmed by a much larger force of the North Vietnamese Army (NVA).

Charlie Company's horrors continued after I was part of them: I was one survivor of yet another terrible battle not too long afterward. I had been dropped into one of the worst places in Vietnam at the worst time. My own combat experiences cover a wide and terrible spectrum. This episode is about one particular ambush that produced my most remarkable experience of all.

About 7–8 months after my arrival in Vietnam, I had transferred from Charlie Company of our Division's 196th Brigade to Delta Company of the Division's 4/21, 11th Infantry Brigade. My "remarkable experience" occurred in one of these two brigades; my repression scrambled the chronology of events and blurred faces.

On "my most remarkable day," I was the "point man" for my company, leading the way along a very well-developed trail in a remote, high mountain rain forest. The trail was carved wide, well worn, and was without any overgrowth of shrubs or vines—a clear sign that the NVA troops were currently using it a lot!" By that time, I had gained much intense combat experience. Experience was the critical attribute for anyone who should walk point in this clearly "hot" NVA territory.

I was always on high alert whenever I walked point. Now in that mode, I suddenly caught a faint odor of cooked rice and sweat; my mind went into hyper-alert! Being able to smell these things meant only one thing: the enemy was very near! In that hyper-alert state, my senses sharpened to an extreme state. My eyes intently zoomed in on every detail within sight, and my ears became like high-tech detectors. At that moment, however, my ears were aware that the only sound I was hearing was *dead silence*— the kind of dead silence known more to outer space than to a very healthy rainforest. It was if the jungle itself was holding its breath in anticipation of an ominous event. All of my previous combat experiences told me that I'd better be extremely ready for what was just ahead!

Within a few tense seconds, the dense tunnel-trail opened up into a large clearing which, unnaturally, had no ground foliage! The lowest 20 feet of this triple canopy jungle had been removed leaving only the higher second and third tree canopies to act as a ceiling that shielded the ground from aerial view. The clearing resembled a living green cathedral but without any altar or pews. The sides of the clearing sloped uphill, creating a long bowl-shaped area.

A few feet into the clearing, I was suddenly aware of rows of thin slot-like windows on both sides of the slopes—shooting slots of North Vietnamese Army bunkers! I had stumbled into an enemy base camp with bunkers dug into the slopes on both sides of me! The only words going through my mind were, "Holy Shit!!!" "Holy Shit!!!" "Holy Shit!!!" It was a heart-stopping sight that flooded me with both controlled terror and body-tingling excitement! My brain cell pathways sizzled!

As per military procedure when encountering such an important situation, I very cautiously backed out of the clearing and then motioned for my RTO (radio operator) to come forward so I could radio to our Company Commander what I had found. A brief pause followed my description, then he radioed back what I fully expected to hear, "Proceed with caution!"

My RTO's eyes were as big as saucers as I told him to quietly pass the word back: "Enemy base-camp!" I then turned and slowly reentered the cleared area. Every hair on my body was standing straight up and adrenaline flowed like a flood. My thumb had long since pushed the small lever of my M-16 rifle from Safety mode to "Fire" mode, and my finger held lightly against the trigger. With each soft, slow step, I scanned every tiny detail of my environment, including where the nearest cover was at any given second. I was certain that something was about to happen at any second, but I felt eerily ready for whatever it would be. All of my previous heavy combat experiences had developed my senses, mental acuity, and combat skills to an extremely high degree—able to will my M-16 to shoot exactly where I looked. My confidence was certainly higher than what was realistic, but I defiantly believed that whatever started, *I* would be able to finish it!

As I slowly crept deeper into the base camp clearing, I knew that other members of my squad were following several yards behind and were now seeing what I first saw. There was absolutely no sound...not our soft footsteps nor deepened breathing...nothing! We took intense care to hear the slightest telltale sign of the enemy.

A very tense couple of minutes passed with no signs of life. The surreal silence promised to be nothing but an illusion of serenity. The cathedral walls of green wrapped around us as if to shield the sweet world outside from what vicious violence were about to be unleashed within.

Then, just as my attention was drawn to a minuscule movement ahead of me, the air *exploded* with machine-gun fire! A camouflaged bunker—directly in front of me—a mere thirty yards away! I was stunned that I had not seen it! However, even more stunning was what followed! So extraordinary it was, that I invariably feel painfully hesitant to tell this part to even close friends and relatives because it's just too incredible for many to accept. Regardless of that feeling, I feel much more hesitant to allow such a personally profound event to go untold! So...here goes.

The Twilight Zone

As is to be expected in combat, gunfire is a norm. I'd been in several ambushes, shot at countless times, and wounded twice already, and my normal reaction was always to instantly return fire while diving to cover. *This time,* however, it was different. Simultaneously with the gunfire, I felt a rapid volley of bullets pound my body all over between my upper right thigh and chest! But instead of returning fire, I became completely peaceful and calm, and amazingly…just *stood* there in awe! Actual time seemed to disappear, and my small section of rainforest felt like a solitary island in the universe.

Then, at the same time that I was feeling the pounding of lead slugs, clear words seemed to fill my entire self and surround me. With a tone of deep reverence, calm gentleness, perfect clarity, and absolute profoundness: *"This is the moment of your death."*

Rather than reacting with any fear, panic, or shock from understanding that I was being shot to death, I felt only absolute calm, acceptance… and total awe. It was a feeling of profoundness that I can only compare to being able to watch yourself being born! Further, I felt like I was watching my life end from slightly behind and above my body at the same time that I was still physically experiencing a pounding assault from inside my body.

What was happening seemed to take *much* longer than the one half to one second that it probably took. It was a total time warp! However, my experience was about to take another amazing turn: another voice then interjected! This time it was a voice that was loud and adamant! The exact words are not clear to me, but the *message* was extremely clear: *"NO, LIVE!!!"*

Immediately, I felt like I was shot out of a cannon and exploded into action! I hurled myself a few feet to my left and aligned my body behind the only nearby cover—a tight clump of three small trees! The trees' meager cover was barely enough to block the stream of bullets that followed me! For a couple of jagged seconds, bullet slugs pummeled the hard wood trunks with sharp, determined "SMACKS!" as I squeezed into a tight rod of flesh and bone to be in safe alignment with my measly cover of little trees!

Then, the air behind me erupted with the sharp "CRACKS" of M-16 rifles as my platoonmates quickly dashed forward into cover and returned fire! The enemy quickly diverted their gunfire from me to my platoon's guns and the air exploded to a *seamless* roar! The echoing dense cathedral walls made it sound like a deafening *indoor* battle!

After several seconds of intense fire, it became obvious that only American M-16's, M-60's, and M-79's were shooting...no more enemy gunfire. Our shooting tapered off as our platoon leader subsequently hollered a command that penetrated through the gunfire, *"Cease fire! Cease fire!"*

The shooting stopped, and there was a moment of near silence with only the fading echo of gunfire to be heard. The previously pristine rainforest air was now a wafting fog of white gun smoke! Again the platoon leader yelled from back the trail, "What do you have up there?!" One of my closest buddies, my RTO, choked out an emotional yell—"They got *Twig!*" Another soldier hollered, "Two or three NVA in a bunker! We got 'em! It looks like they're the only dinks here!"

As I lay behind the small tree clump, I felt like a voiceless *spectator*. I "knew" that I was mortally wounded and near death if not dead. My mind was filled with the sensation of pounding bullets...and that "profound pronouncement of my death!" It felt like I was only seeing what was happening around me via some kind of "after-death awareness" or something.

The platoon leader then hollered the command, "Spread out to give cover and get the medic down there!" As the platoon leader continued to direct each squad into strategically maneuvered guard positions, my RTO buddy arose and began approaching in a "crouched defensive posture," but slowly and hesitantly, as if his heart didn't *really* want to see what he knew he was going to find! As he got closer, his eyes were scanning my body. When he finally got to me, his eyes widened, and he spoke in an incredulous but slightly hopeful tone, "Twig? You alive?!" He knelt beside me and looked at—*no* bloody wounds!...*None!!!*

He reached down and put his hand behind my upper arm and repeated, "Twig?!" Though I was clearly hearing and seeing, I still felt as unable to speak as a dead man. However, on the hope that maybe I still possessed a small amount of life, and with a compelling "morbid curiosity," I lowered my eyes downward, fully expecting to see the horrible bullet wounds that my RTO had also expected to see. My eyes probably widened and blinked in disbelief as I too saw...*no blood!*

Seeing my eyes blink, he blurted, "Twig, you're alive!" Then with an incredulous tone, he stammered, "I mean...I mean...it looks...looks like you're *not even wounded!* Are you okay?!" Having also just seen my "impossibly intact" body, I choked out a quiet, confused, "I don't know... I felt bullets hitting me!" Now giddy in disbelief, he immediately agreed, "I know! I thought they were shooting the shit out of you!!!" He had been less than 10 yards behind me when the enemy gunners opened up, and he thought he saw my body being pounded! We were both stunned, and our minds reeled to comprehend what just happened! What surely seemed to have happened...*didn't!*

"TWIG'S ALIVE," he hollered as he sat me up against the trees! The medic had made it down the trail and was hurriedly approaching us. My RTO buddy looked up at him and exclaimed, "He's alive! I don't think he's even wounded!" The entire platoon in the area, passed the news back up the trail, "Twig's alive! He's okay!!!" Whoops of relief echoed throughout the cathedral walls! Despite NVA's perfectly set up ambush, I had somehow survived!

Later, after my company had secured the area and ascertained that the two dead NVA had indeed been the only ones there, we paused for our C-ration lunch and our platoon gathered around me and my RTO. There was lots of celebratory joking and excited discussion as my RTO and I recounted the incredible event: a perfect ambush; two NVA soldiers in a well-camouflaged bunker only 30 yards away; their machine-gun sights held tightly on me, the point man, and then they *missed!* Unbelievable!

My mind would often replay the event thereafter. I felt deeply bewildered. I kept asking myself, "What the heck happened back there?! How could I feel pounding bullets...and that clear voice that announced my death???!!! Everything that had happened earlier seemed absolutely clear and real!!! *Surreal,* actually. I felt like I was a part of a *"Twilight Zone"* movie.

Of course, like you, I also can't help but wonder, "Did all those bullets actually miss me in that ambush despite their virtually point-blank range?! Did my mind merely present me with a lifelike "illusion" of being pounded by slugs and hearing a crystal-clear proclamation of my death?" I have a strong college background in both science and psychology. I have scrutinized all possibilities with passionate analytical rigor in the years since, and my honest conclusion is, "I just don't know."

That I was retrieved from death seems too incredible for even me to believe myself! However, what I can say for certain: (1) The bullet impacts felt morbidly real; (2) The words that I heard were every bit as clear as if I were hearing them through surround-sound speakers in this room; (3) I experienced a state of profoundness that I'd never felt before or since; (4) I felt like I was viewing the event from outside of my body, and; (5) My RTO also thought that I was being pounded by the machine gun bullets!

In the end, it turned out that those two North Vietnamese Army soldiers stayed behind their regiment as "rear guard"—alone, to stall us during their regiment's escape! Their rear-guard was a suicide mission, a highly noble assignment for the two young NVA! And, even though their mission was to kill me and as many GI's as possible, I, as a fellow infantryman and human being, can't help but feel strong respect for their heroism in the face of certain death. They would have had no doubt that they would end up being shot to death.

Strangely, I had felt that I too had died during their ambush. It is not without unease that I will now admit that part of me *still* believes that somehow I did die at that extraordinary moment in 1968...and then, somehow, got to be alive again. Yes, I know that sounds wacky to most people and even to myself! But it also seems just as preposterous that I *wouldn't get shot at all* from such close range! What I experienced is just too profound for me to ignore! I am left with the thought that life is actually much more mysterious than we think!

A former science teacher, I'm still a certified "science nerd." I've analyzed that event from the perspective of quantum physics to explain it. But, who knows! I just know that I experienced something disturbingly mysterious back then. And it still haunts me.

In recording this event, I couldn't help but wonder if, at the moment of their death, the two North Vietnamese soldiers experienced the same mysterious things that I did at "my own moment." Do all of us, when we actually die, have similar mysterious experiences but don't return to our bodies to tell about it? Whatever the reality, I remain in awe of that event which I can only label a "near-death experience." I feel frustrated that, right now, I just can't be sure of what is "reality" and what is not.

Everyone has his or her own beliefs about what happens after death. If my own belief about a spiritual world proves true, I will learn the answer to these questions when my "*irreversible* time" to die comes. Then, maybe, I'll even be able to meet those two NVA rear-guard souls, *not* as enemies, but as two individuals meeting face to face…man to man; infantryman to infantryman; human spirit to human spirit…in total peace. And then, finally, I might learn the reality of "what the heck happened back there?!"

THE SUBTERRANEAN NVA WORLD

FOR THE REST OF THAT DAY, my company carefully searched and explored the NVA base camp that we had found. It was a spectacular underground village and amazingly engineered and excavated. However, our entering into the NVA underground complex through one of the small entrance holes had a very dangerous potential! There was no way of knowing if any more "rear guard" enemy soldiers were down there. I was the first to volunteer to go down into the subsurface world of the enemy. A couple other volunteer "tunnel rats" followed after I called in and said that it looked uninhabited. As a tunnel rat, one feels extremely vulnerable to leave the safety and sight of his company and slip down into an unknown darkness!

Below ground, the NVA "hallways" and rooms were only about three to five feet high so we had to explore it crawling on our hands and knees. We cautiously inched our way with our .45 caliber pistols readied in our right hand, and army flashlights in our left. The air inside was very humid and heavy and smelled strongly of humans, so we fully expected that we could encounter NVA occupants. We never knew if an enemy lay waiting in one of the several rooms, ready to blow our heads off when we entered. Surprisingly, we encountered no NVA down there, nor did we find any when we searched the surrounding jungle! The NVA regiment had escaped!

However, we were also extremely apprehensive of booby-traps that the NVA may have set for us! Most veterans of war would agree that they fear booby-traps more than bullets any day! However, this NVA evacuation must have been too rushed to have time to set any traps! Whew!!!

Those of us who volunteered as "tunnel rats" to search the underground city felt intense excitement. It produced a heavy pump of adrenaline! As scary as it was, I also felt total *awe* of the NVA's alien world! It was the sight of a lifetime, an experience that will be indelibly engrained in every tunnel rat's mind forever!

As it turned out, the underground complex was built under the entire aboveground clearing and beyond. There were tunnels extending up to the defensive bunkers which had their "shooting slots" that I had first observed. Down in their subterranean village, we discovered dozens of small rooms and several large cavernous rooms supported by pillars of poles and dirt-packed tree roots. There were several large, communal sleeping rooms where platoon-size groups of soldiers slept. There were also individual sleeping quarters (for officers?), some with interesting peppery and incense-like odors. All sleeping areas had woven mats on the ground, which served as very simple "beds."

We also found a large hospital chamber with better padded mats. That chamber had a smell of alcohol, as well as a "sick" smell of infection. Nearby was also a colorful Buddhist chapel with colored ribbons, candles, and a raised dirt altar with a fancy-woven straw mat on top. But no Buddha: escapees apparently took their Buddha statue when they fled. I respect that; in war especially, spirituality can be a saving grace.

There was also an armory that still had weapons and ammunition in it! The valuable cache must have been more than they could take in their very *hasty* evacuation! And, perhaps most telling of the NVA's panicked flight, there was the camp's large, candle-lit cafeteria where rice still sat on their plates! Candles and small oil lamps still burned their dim light throughout the complex—one more clear and spooky proof that this regimental base camp had been occupied only short minutes before we arrived!

As I write this, I now recall that at some time during my 416 days in Vietnam—perhaps during this encounter with the NVA—I discovered two young NVA nurses hiding in dense foliage just a few feet off a jungle trail. This certainly could have been during the same event as described above; my mental image of those nurses' hiding places matches my memory of the underground camp area. I do remember that the two young women looked even tougher than they looked scared! I often wonder if American Intelligence personnel treated those nurses well after we flew them back to Americal Division for interrogation. I hope so; they probably had a tough life...living most of their time underground taking care of sick and wounded. And I'm certain that they were an important part of the large NVA camp that I found.

From the beginning, the encampment "screamed of life." Our search had to be done appropriately slow! Going down into a subterranean base camp such as this one was extremely dangerous! In my opinion, every man who served as a tunnel rat digging into fresh underground base camps deserves a military's Soldiers Medal *awarded for bravery in a non-combat action.* Luckily, although this subterranean camp was occupied minutes earlier, it turned out that there was nothing left except the haunting and powerful imagery of what life was like for a North Vietnamese soldier!

It was an exciting and exhilarating experience for an infantryman! And I had thought that all enemy-related experiences were going to be bad ones. Some things in Vietnam were just plain *cool!*

FIREFIGHT IN AN ARTILLERY BARRAGE

 in Vietnam was a horrible battle in which my infantry company was grossly outnumbered and was completely overrun. From that infantry company of about 120 men, I was one of those who survived to return to combat afterward. My experience was so terrifying that it had stayed almost completely shielded from memory for over forty years!

I was able to drag much of this battle out of repression in 2003 *only* in the psychological security of the psych ward of the Boise, Idaho Veterans Hospital where I had voluntarily gone for treatment for post-traumatic stress disorder (PTSD). This was an intensive six-week inpatient program that was set up to treat four of the worst cases of combat PTSD from the northwest region of the United States. I was extremely fortunate to be put at the front of their application line due to the strong lobbying of my terrific veterans' counselor, Tony Rizzo. Since my PTSD had forced early retirement in 2002, I had been traveling from my Helena, Montana home up to Great Falls to get Tony's help.

My PTSD had been ignited in 1995 by the overwhelming combined stresses of the murder of my youngest brother, of being a high school counselor, and the painful break-up of a great relationship. The intensity of dealing with all three major stressors at once "broke the dam" that had locked away virtually all of my Vietnam traumas. The dam break unleashed a massive deluge of pent-up violent emotions and experiences

that had severely impaired my mental functioning. Efforts to recuperate from that horrible year failed despite my most sincere efforts. Consequently, I staggered into an early retirement—very badly in need of finally getting war-related counseling.

In the decades prior to my getting help at the Boise VA, the only memories I had of this horrible battle were recurring "floating film segments" of images that were incomplete and disconnected. They had spontaneously popped into my mind ever since my return from Vietnam. Included in this film reel was a three second image of terrifying roars and crashes from a vicious nighttime artillery barrage a very dangerous fifty yards in front of me! Menacing, jagged shrapnel from the explosions shredded the triple canopy jungle overhead causing leaves and branches to fall all around me. Frustratingly, every time this image popped into my head, I could never recall any more of the story of what *had* to have been an insanely horrible situation! I always wondered how I could possibly *not* remember that whole battle!

In the psychological safety of the Boise PTSD treatment program, I dared to systematically delve into the rest of that horrible battle. Superb counselors and specially trained staff were always very nearby throughout the long, intense days and nights. There, I joined three other seriously traumatized war veterans. We bunked in the same room on the hospital's psych ward, and gave vital support and insights for each other during our daily group therapy sessions.

Therapy and PTSD

For the first four weeks of treatment—despite my sincerest efforts—my mind stubbornly limited my recall to only a few non-threatening pieces of the entry into this haunting battle. Simple pieces of the early part of the battle returned. There was an image of my infantry company coming under enemy fire as we descended a mountain jungle trail into a shallow saddle late one cloudy afternoon. I also recalled myself returning fire while I lay prone behind a large tree. However, these two additional memories were too scant to be useful. I continued to struggle in vain to remember the *whole* battle!

Then, a breakthrough! Around 3:00 A.M. on April 14, 2003, I lay in restless pre-sleep in my Boise VA bed with the partial scenes of that terrible artillery barrage playing over and over in my mind. Suddenly my heart leapt when I thought that I was hearing my infantry platoon sergeant frantically screaming, "Get your heads up! Get your head up!!! They're running over the top of us!!!"

In a heart-stopping extremely realistic flashback, I was back in Vietnam hugging the bottom of a foxhole that I had dug behind the tree. Terrifying shards of artillery shrapnel shredded the jungle around me! "Hearing" my platoon sergeant's warning instantly jolted the battle scene back into memory! Important new pieces of the long-repressed battle flooded back into my mind! The battle was suddenly and *vividly* "happening again!"

Graphic segments of the furious battle flashed frighteningly clear in front of my eyes: NVA soldiers sprinting past the tree behind which I had my camouflaged foxhole! Then came the image of an *electrically* charged image of me shooting two NVA soldiers three feet away!!!

An instant later, "some other horror" started to reveal at the *left* side of my tree! I can only describe it as "some other horror" because, before my mind could reveal what it was, my flashback suddenly burst! I bolted upright in my bed!! My heart was pounding out of my chest and I gasped for air! The image of whatever was about to happen at the left side of my tree popped my flashback like a giant balloon! My wide eyes abruptly switched from seeing violent combat to the surreal contrast of my dark hospital room! My mind reeled with confusion! The flashback was so vivid that I found myself grasping wildly for whatever it was that was actually real—the combat or the room!

Suddenly my heart jumped back to near panic level at the sound of my platoon sergeant screaming again…except that "the sergeant's screaming" was actually coming from one of the other guys in my hospital room! Technically, my roommate was not screaming but coughing wildly during an asthma attack! The high pitch of his long coughs matched the pitch of my platoon sergeant's frantic screams of alarm! That *stark similarity* tricked my mind into believing that it was my infantry platoon sergeant's voice, and it triggered the flashback of my long-repressed battle scene!

I sat in my bed very shaken! My mind raced from its shocking release of the battle scene memory. The whole purpose of my being in this VA hospital was to uncover treacherously repressed memories, so I felt great frustration that the *complete* recall of this important battle had been thwarted by my awakening! I lay myself back down and tried to coax the battle flashback to return for completion. I had a strong feeling that the still-hidden "event at left side of my tree" was a deeper trauma that greatly fueled my disabling PTSD!

I replayed my new recollections of the battle over and over in hopes that the battle's continuation would naturally occur. The result was only great exasperation. My best attempts to force the memory of the battle failed. So, I got up, put my robe on and rushed down the hall to our group's "writing/processing room." There, I wrote every detail that I could remember about the flashback! As I sat rapidly writing, another segment of the battle spontaneously tumbled back into my consciousness. Then another, and another…one-by-one…until a more complete picture of the horrible battle started to take shape. Alone in the night, I wrote furiously, and the writing process further stimulated more recall of the repressed battle. Basically, I was *reliving* the battle as I wrote!

I was sickened and horrified as other elusive scenes of the battle returned! That night of the attack on my company was an experience that absolutely went off the charts of my *own* "horror scale!" Below are the portions of the battle that returned to my heart-pounding consciousness as I wrote that night.

The Battle

I'll start at the beginning of the battle. Earlier, in the afternoon before the night of the battle, our company had been trailing what we knew was a large force of NVA. I was among the first few guys in the company's lead. We had just descended a gradually sloping trail through a triple canopy jungle and had started to cross an open, sparsely vegetated saddle on the mountain.

Suddenly, a roar of gunfire erupted from the up-slope in front of us! It was a huge ambush! Survivors scattered for the nearest cover and a fierce firefight ensued! My cover was behind a three-foot wide tree in the bottom of that saddle. The first eight or ten of us lay about fifteen to twenty feet apart. Most of our company was shooting right over our heads from their positions on the up-slope behind us!

Some time into the fight, I became alarmingly aware that sounds of AK-47 rifle fire were coming at us from both sides! Ominously, this meant that the NVA were attempting a double flanking maneuver, which would expose us to a deadly crossfire! The cover of our trees, which had barely provided cover from the *frontal* fire, would soon be nullified! I yelled this imminent danger to the rest of our platoon! It became vital that we somehow increase our protection from bullets that would soon be coming from our sides! The subsequent command from our combat experienced platoon sergeant rang out, "Dig in!!!"

The enemy's heavy rifle and machine gun fire made digging a foxhole extremely dangerous! Barrages of bullets were smacking against our trees and kicking up dirt inches away! Any lateral movement at all would expose our bodies to being hit. My shovel was in my pack only a couple feet to my left. I had shed the pack to be able to return fire with agility from a prone position. Reaching for my shovel was too dangerous, so I pressed myself into a sitting position tight behind my tree and frantically started to plow a trench in the soft humus with my boot heels. Simultaneously having to return fire, my excavation felt excruciatingly slow as I heard enemy rifle fire extending further to our flanks!

Soon, however, I was able to slide down into the trench that my boot heels had created. I then began deepening the front of it with my sturdy K-bar knife and hands until I had a four-foot deep foxhole behind and partially under the tree. The battle raged on as darkness descended.

Wanting to make my position as invisible as possible to the enemy in a prolonged battle, I refilled the rear portion of my initial trench with dirt excavated from the foxhole. I stealthily flung small handfuls of excavated dirt away from my new foxhole to eliminate any *telltale* mound around myself. I then added strategic camouflage by sticking sliced plant branches into the soil around me. Finally, I had a *very* well-disguised defensive position from which to return fire!

Dangerously, the triple canopy prevented our getting critical air support because we weren't visible from the air even during the day! It was futile to signal our position by popping smoke grenades as we usually did. Fighting continued into the night as artillery-fired parachute flares burst above the triple canopy and provided thin rays of penetrating light. It wasn't very illuminating, but at least we'd be able to see any enemy maneuvers.

Meanwhile, I was dreadfully aware that our unfortunate position at the front of the firefight was made even more deadly because the rest of our platoon was shooting *just inches over our heads* from behind us. We *front liners* would inadvertently get shot by our own guys if it suddenly became necessary for us to jump up and move! We were pinned down from both directions!

The enemy was as close as 120 feet, so it was no surprise when grenades exploded around us at the front. But I noticed that the sound of some of the grenade blasts were from GI grenades! They were preceded by a wooden "thock" above us, so I quickly deduced that our men behind us were lobbing grenades that were hitting obscured vines in the dark canopy above us. Those grenades then dropped straight down onto those of us in the front! Intense firefight is always horrible enough, but the danger from "friendly fire" is a very real, even more tragic hazard! I can't say if any American-thrown grenades killed or wounded any of us in the front! That part of the battle is still repressed.

Much larger explosions soon roared when a withering American artillery barrage was called in on the enemy to break their deadly stronghold. Perhaps for the first part of our battle, it was feared that the shielding thick overhead canopy and the enemy's close proximity to us made artillery too precarious! Now, however, a desperate strategy was employed. The first rounds detonated about 500 yards behind the enemy. Word was relayed to us that "other artillery rounds would be 'walked closer and closer' to us until they were exploding in the near NVA positions...so everyone *get down!!!*" I will say, unequivocally, that there is no more terrifying sound than artillery rounds roaring in and detonating at close range! First you hear an increasingly loud, *screaming/buzzing/crackling* roar coming nearer...then, a deafening, crunching *"BOOM!!!"*

Quickly, the vicious artillery blasts came to within only 100 yards... then to a horrifying fifty yards. My flesh had never felt so pathetically fragile! Artillery pounded right on top of the NVA's front positions and but nearly right on top of *us* too. It was extremely terrifying! Large, spinning, jagged blades of red-hot iron rocketed out from each detonated round and shredded swaths of jungle around us! We all pressed tightly into the deepest recesses of our foxholes! I retreated partially under my tree, among its roots! Artillery-slashed branches of all sizes and a snowstorm of leaves rained down on us!

All of us hunkered deep—everyone except our brave, battle-wise old platoon sergeant! He kept vigil despite being exposed to the deadly artillery barrage. His lengthy experience told him that, with *nobody* watching, we were vulnerable to another risk beyond the artillery, a ground attack!

And that is exactly what happened minutes later! Many NVA were being hacked and blown apart as the withering artillery blasts rained right on top of them, to their sides, and to their rear! To survive eventual annihilation, the NVA troops were apparently given the brilliant strategic order to rise and dash to where there were no artillery blasts, which was ahead of where *we were!* Upon seeing the artillery-flash silhouettes of NVA soldiers charging toward us, our platoon sergeant immediately screamed, "Get your heads up! Get your heads up, they're coming over the top of us!!!"

The fast charging NVA didn't start shooting until they had penetrated into our midst then began firing rifle bursts into every foxhole they saw as they ran! Along with the roar of the artillery blasts, the night suddenly filled with the terrifying sound of enemy AK-47's and enraged screams of hordes of charging NVA soldiers all around us!!!

Immediately thrusting my eyes to near the surface behind my tree, I was aghast to see enemy soldiers shooting down into foxholes of GI's about 30 and 40 feet to my left! I was just about to open fire on them when more NVA charged past my tree only a couple feet to my right!!! I barely readied my M-16 when another screaming NVA came charging behind them, shooting at the GI's behind me, clearly oblivious to me in my camouflaged position behind the tree right in front of him! I got my M-16 up in time to fire a "full automatic" burst into him at point-blank range! And a quarter second later…another NVA! Before he was able to swing his aim all the way at me, I ripped an instantly lethal point-blank burst into him too—from his heart to head!

Swarms of enemy soldiers flooded through the jungle at us! My company returned fire in a deafening blizzard of bullets! The firefight erupted into an insane all-out-war! NVA everywhere. Gunfights at a range of four feet. Exploding artillery rounds near us becoming secondary dangers! It was 100% raw PANIC!!! Insane levels of screaming and yelling and shooting!!! A million things seemed to be happening at once! Every rule of war, religion, and humanity was instantly obliterated! The *non*-rules of *total* chaos took over!!!

Suddenly, amid this overwhelming chaos, *"something"* then appeared at the left side of my tree!!! My panicked eyes and rifle barrel instantly slashed left to respond.

In an instant, the wild recall of my chaotic battle immediately screeched to an abrupt halt...*again!!!* My exhumed battle scenes instantly scattered into the protective darkness of my mind like panicked little animals dashing for cover when vicious wolves suddenly pounce into their midst!

My mind had been *absolutely* consumed by my wild, startling memory. But now I was suddenly jolted back to the reality of the brightly lit writing room where I had been furiously documenting! Damn!!! That *"left of tree"* event screech-halted my memory again in the same way that it had during the flashback in my hospital bed. This frustrated the hell out of me!

I desperately tried to force my mind to replay that battle sequence by visualizing all the graphic details of that moment! My conscious mind battered at the concrete walls of my subconscious mind's repression fortress! The walls stubbornly held! Damn it! Damn it!!! I needed the critical *full* details of that battle in order to slay my dragon! The emotional intensity of that still hidden "something" at the left of my foxhole/tree was apparently more than my mind could handle! "Bullshit, you damned subconscious! Give me the truth!" I just couldn't imagine how that *"something"* could be so much worse than what I was already recalling that it still needed protective shielding!

Despite extraordinary psychological resistance, I forced my mind back into that battle and was able to successfully drag still more pieces out of hiding. However, they were only disjointed images from near the end of battle and its aftermath! Here are additional images that came back into my head.

Images Out of Hiding

The Foxhole

The first image out of hiding was of me lying on my back in my foxhole, with my body and my M-16 helplessly pinned beneath the weight of a lifeless body that was sitting on my chest. One of his legs was twisted around under my back so that our combined weight pressed his boot edge *hard* between my shoulder blades! Blood from his body was drenching me. Despite great pain, I felt forced to remain motionless as I heard NVA soldiers going around "snuffing foxholes" with deadly AK-47 rifle bursts! Their obvious intention: complete extermination of our horribly over-matched company! A desperate idea flashed into my terrified mind. Able to move my right forearm and hand only slightly, I managed to put some of the drenching blood into my right eye socket. I dabbed a small pinch of dirt into the center of the blood pool to make it look like a lethally dark bloody bullet hole. My only escape from sure death!

The Soldier with the AK-47

The next image to the surface was the soldier. A young NVA soldier had found my camouflaged foxhole and was aiming his AK-47 down at me as I lay motionless in the bottom of my foxhole! Then his wild, angry expression unexpectedly softened, and he left *without* shooting...his eyes tracking my face as he disappeared from view. I'm haunted by the question of whether he thought that I was already mortally wounded or dead, or if he chose to spare me out of pity?! There seemed to be some kind of unspoken communication with me before he left me alive.

The Silence and Panic

Along with the soldier, came the memory of silence and panic. As the NVA had apparently finished their bloody work and seemingly left the area, a deathly silence ensued. Minutes later, I felt sudden *panic* when the silence was broken by a near-death GI's *moaning!* It was *incessant* and *much too audible.* I desperately wanted to shush him: the NVA might still be near enough to hear him and come back! With terrible frustration, I had to remain absolutely silent and motionless! I could only *"scream"* at him silently inside my frantic mind, "Shut up, you crazy fool. Shut up! They'll return to kill *everyone* who might still be alive." Please shut up!!! SHUT UP!!!"

The Darkness

After the silence and panic came the darkness. Long after the GI's moaning had finally stopped (he probably died), there was pitch black. I lay in my dark foxhole, still not moving except for mindlessly clenching and unclenching my fists against thick sticky blood that filled my hands. This mindless action made a barely audible smacking sound each time I relaxed my fists. "Smack—smack—smack." I think that I may have been doing it to provide a tiny bit of "living company" for myself during the painful solitude of that interminably long night. I felt like a man adrift and alone in the stark darkness of deep space.

I was so numb with shock that I wasn't sure if I too had been wounded in the same chaos that put the dead GI in my foxhole with me! My head and back ached like crazy! Did a grenade kill the GI and wound me too? I couldn't be sure of any of that.

Survival Instinct

Another image out of hiding was that of survival. My mind stumbled for a way to somehow get out of this alive. My survival instinct scolded away any thought of giving up! As I calmed my mind to consider all possible scenarios, many horrible barriers became apparent! I was dreadfully aware that I may be the only survivor; there were absolutely no sounds of life around me. I may not be able to survive the countless uncertainties of being alone in NVA territory when daylight finally comes! I mean, which way would I safely go? It seemed like the NVA left in the same direction from which we came! I couldn't dare yell out for help because the NVA may be the only ones to hear me! Where am I in relation to any GI base camp? I had no clue! I felt painfully, desperately, *hopelessly* lost!

Dead Weight

Piece by piece, the memories came back. Next in queue was that of the foxhole and the grave. As I lay in hiding, I wasn't even certain that I would be able to extricate myself from beneath the dead soldier on top of me in my narrow foxhole! My only way out would be to somehow push his dead weight up and over the edge of my foxhole. He felt so heavy, and I felt so weakened in my awkward, cramped position! As such, the dreaded ironic possibility was that my foxhole, so cleverly engineered to provide life-giving sanctuary, might now become my *grave!*

The Faint Light of Morning

Accompanying the image of the foxhole came the memory of light. I recalled—after being pinned in the foxhole for what seemed like an eternity—that, *finally,* the first faint light of morning appeared!!! Shortly, my heart leapt to life upon hearing the distant sound of *American* voices echoing through the damp jungle!! Another infantry company was coming to look for any possible survivors!!! I probably made muffled attempts at calling out; I can't remember for sure. Soon, I looked up to see the face of a young GI looking down at me in the bottom of my foxhole. His expression turned to a huge smile as he recognized life! "Medic," he hollered! "There's one alive over here!" Soon GI's carefully lifted me out! I groaned while being examined...feeling *bone-wracking pain* from my being crunched to the bottom of my foxhole during that endless night with a boot edge dug into my back!

Someone Else's Blood

A final image that came out of hiding was that of blood. Other GI's gathered around and learned to their amazement that none of the blood that caked my body was mine! It was *all* from the body on top of me. Whomever the body belonged to, his blood very likely made me look dead enough to keep me from being "snuffed" by the rampaging NVA. Though I eventually left Vietnam with three separate wounds, I escaped being seriously wounded in this battle except for a possible concussion which left my head feeling swollen and aching badly. *All* of me ached like hell!

I remember crying, and I have sometimes cried when remembering this…even forty years later.

Staring Down Pandora and Surviving

The preceding images are the only parts of the horrific battle that I could drag from my mind's steel vault of repression, and their retrieval was made possible only by the therapeutic safety of the Boise Veterans Hospital. The memory came out very begrudgingly. It absolutely didn't want to stand naked in the daylight!

It still frustrates me that the *whole* battle memory refuses to come back. What happened at the left side of that tree?! That "something" was obviously horrible enough to still remain shielded from my conscious awareness since 1968. Though it feels like an important part of my PTSD, perhaps remembering it would evoke a terror, guilt, or grief that could still be beyond my ability to cope. Since the Boise VA treatment, I *feel* like I could handle and forgive anything that my subconscious mind coughs up...no matter how painful!

My gut tells me that *"the something"* had to do with the dead man who ended up on my chest during that horrific night. Who was he?! I can only believe that he must have been one of our guys because the NVA retrieved their own dead whenever possible. How did the guy die? Bullets, grenade, artillery shrapnel? By NVA bullets or from the bullets of fellow GI's shooting from behind us? Or, worst of all, was it from *my* bullets during the extreme chaos of the moment?! (Please, God...not that)!

Perhaps, he left his own foxhole during the overwhelming attack and ran to my foxhole so as not have to die alone and was killed as he jumped in. Perhaps it was a grenade blast that killed him and knocked me out...and that grenade blast was the *something* that occurred in my unconsciousness. This scenario seems plausible! My mind is racing to make sense of *the something*...an explanation without involving *me* shooting my own guy!

It also just occurred to me that those GI's who came during the first light after the battle may have been remnants of my own company! Perhaps some our own guys survived the ground attack by pulling back into the cover of the thick jungle, and then returned at daylight to retrieve bodies/survivors! Maybe then, my company actually had dozens of survivors. I do remember that my company was taken out of action (Stand-Down) for a period afterward until we had replaced our dead and soldiers who were too wounded to return to combat. Too much repression still keeps much of that battle blurry. I am haunted by many questions still! More damn questions than answers.

Perhaps, however, I don't really need to know more. Perhaps, at Boise I learned the main thing that was *critical,* that I am now strong enough to look directly into the face of mythology's mighty Pandora and not "turn to stone!" I did not die nor forever lose my mind! *The* fear of losing my mind was a *real* fear for me, and I think, might have been the main fuel behind my disabling PTSD. This hypothesis feels like it fits, and it noticeably lessens my anxiety as I contemplate it!

Whatever the answers may be, whenever I focus on that terrible night, I often get a sick feeling in my stomach and a nagging pain between my shoulder blades…right where the dead soldier's boot heavily pressed. So, I realize that my life-saving PTSD therapy at the Boise VA didn't leave me "all cured." And soldiers like me may *never* be *all cured.* But I'm *all cured enough!* My life is full of richness and blessings beyond what I could ever had hoped for when lying in that foxhole! I am now happy, mostly functional, and fully alive. In some ways, I'm even better for my ordeals.

There is a saying that is useful to remember: "Shit happens." Life is usually not shit-free for us human beings. But every elephant on Earth shit on us that night! Yes, I can still get a whiff of all of that elephant shit now and then. However, rather than fight the memory, I now try to accept it as a friendly reminder that I was one of the lucky ones to survive some of the worst combat shit possible. I am living. My life was allowed to continue after the insane firefight in an artillery barrage.

WAR CRIMES—THE UGLIEST PART OF A WAR

WAR IS NEVER PRETTY! However, there were times when it is flat out and undeniably ugly. Among those times are when lawless soldiers lose their moral compass and commit atrocities against humanity.

My purpose here is not to judge my fellow soldiers, but to simply illustrate how combat circumstances can unleash a horrible darkness within man. I would like to state first, that *all* wars have some war crimes. I would also like to state that, for soldiers who *witness* war crimes, it is not nearly as easy for them to report the crimes as people who have never been in armed combat would think. By that I mean:

- The concepts of teamwork, obedience, and loyalty are fiercely in-grained during military training to build *tight-knit* bands of troops who will stick together for survival during combat.
- Decent men can eventually get so caught up in the ugliness of war that *extremely ugly* begins to feel normal!
- Desperate sleep deficiency + extreme fear, rage, or grief = damaged decision-making.
- Those who commit war crimes might be men who are fighting beside you. They are men upon whom your own life might depend... and who could silence you with one "accidental" bullet!
- "Higher-ups," who receive any crime reports, will sometimes punish *reporters* of the crimes rather than those who commit the crime!

All of these are powerful forces that can operate inside *good* soldiers' minds. Despite those powerful forces, we in honorable societies must realize and demand that the ultimate loyalty of our military must be to humanity! Most of our troops served fiercely but under the rules of the Geneva Convention. Below are some of the evils of war that I saw.

The Girl

Let me first start with two events in which I was very nearly victimized by the war criminals. The first event happened at a small, scattered farming community at the edge of the jungle. My platoon's orders were to spread out and go from hut to hut and stable to stable in search of hidden weapons. After a while, I happened to go into one of the outlying huts, and to my great dismay, I found two of my squadmates in the process of stripping a teenage Vietnamese girl! A third soldier, their buddy from another squad, was restraining the girl's pleading mother while the other two held the girl's arms and pulled at her clothes.

I couldn't believe my eyes, and demanded, "What the *hell* are you guys doing?!" One of them responded with a grin, "We're doing a 'titty check'! You know…to see if her shoulders have any bruises from firing rifles. Then we are going to "get a little boom-boom" (sex)! You can join us if you want." I exclaimed, "Bull shit, man! You can't do that! That's rape!"

My words wiped the silly grins off their faces, but the one who was restraining the mother countered with a terse, "Shit, you know as well as we do that these are all Viet Cong in this area, and we deserve to have a little fun! If you don't want any, you don't have to, but don't try to stop us from having some fun!"

I was blessed to have been raised with a sense of morality so, of course, I wasn't buying that crap! Moving toward them, I firmly stated that I wouldn't allow them to commit the rape! At that point, the one who was restraining the mother (I'll call him Tot) let go of the mother and calmly acted as if he was going to comply. He casually picked up his M-16 rifle as if he were going to head out, but suddenly, he quickly raised his M-16 and aimed it at right at my face, "You try to stop us and I'll blow your fucking head off!"

The other two guys, who happened to be in my squad, squirmed at how dangerous the situation quickly became and stopped undressing the young girl. "Hey, come on, man," one of them weakly said to Tot, "this ain't worth this shit. Come on...let's go." Yeah, man," added the other, "let's get out of here."

Unfortunately, Tot was a classic alpha type, and he was enraged that I was interfering! "Keep going," he growled at them, "This asshole isn't going to stop us!" Glaring at me with an evil smile on his face, "You make a single move, and this rifle is going to 'accidentally go off,' and no one will ever know what really happened."

Tot's fiery eyes were firmly locked onto mine. And, although his buddies continued to squirm and plead with him, Tot's eyes suggested that he was crazy enough to do exactly what he said he would! He refused to back off! It clearly looked like I was going to be forced into a "lose-lose" situation in which I would either have to watch an innocent girl get raped, or try to prevent it and maybe get killed by a lunatic!

I didn't know what I was going to do, but I *knew* I couldn't stand and watch them rape that girl! Then incredible good fortune intervened! A barely audible clatter of military gear sounded somewhere outside this hut. Another GI was in the area! Knowing that Tot had heard it too, my mind raced to seize a golden opportunity. I bellowed, "If your gun goes off, Tot, it won't be an accident!!!"

Tot's eyes darted to the door of the hut and then back to me! Then his crazed eyes narrowed, and a horrible, sneering smile came over his face! He knew I had thwarted his evil rape plan. "Don't think this is over," he said as he clicked his rifle back to safety mode. I slapped the barrel of his rifle away from my face! My heart was pounding, and I was mad enough to kill him! Another potentially deadly confrontation ensued as I shoved him hard as he walked past me towards the door. His two buddies (my own squadmates), dashed between us and out the door. I could tell that they were deeply appalled and scared by what had just happened! Tot was their buddy but I was their squadmate—conflicting loyalties. And they had been smack dab in the middle of what could have destroyed all of our of lives (and that of the young Vietnamese girl's and her mother)...all because of unbridled lust, their blurred rules of war, and a lack of human decency.

Frustratingly, my mind has repressed how things turned out for those three guys and me after that. However, I'm sure that because Tot had threatened, "Don't think this is over," I probably reported the situation to our platoon leader to prevent myself from getting "accidentally" shot by Tot during a later battle. Tot may have consequently been sent either to the stockade or transferred to a different unit. It's also possible that, in the insanity of war, we all just "moved past it" and tried to survive battles and go home alive.

The Old Man

The second war crime that nearly cost me my life, was at the hands of another one of my platoonmates. At that time, I was a sergeant and squad leader. My battalion was on a dangerous sweep through a village area that was reportedly occupied by a large mass of NVA troops. The day before this mission, pamphlets had been dropped by airplanes telling the civilians to "Get out, we are coming in! *Anyone still present will be considered hostile forces!*" Battalion Intelligence indicated that an intense battle was ahead.

My duty was to "bring up the rear" to provide a rear guard to assure that none of our men got left behind. The shooting ahead of me was still relatively light as I moved cautiously forward on the outskirts of the village. Just ahead, I saw one of my platoonmates step back from a grenade explosion in one of the civilians' protective bunkers. As I got closer, I could see a human figure crawling from the smoky entrance; it looked like a thin Vietnamese man. The GI, with M-16 aimed, kicked the now kneeling man in the face and was yelling menacingly at him! Wary of the seeming fact that the GI had captured an enemy, I cautiously closed in.

As I got near, however, I could see that the man was actually a very old civilian peasant who was pleading with his hands pressed together prayer-like! The GI butt-stroked him in the head, and the old man went down again. I was appalled because I could see that the man was so old and frail that he obviously was not an enemy combatant, and he probably assumed that he was safe to stay home!

I told the GI (I'll call him "Strike") to "stop and move on…that it's just a harmless old man!" He yelled back that leaflets proclaimed that "only hostiles" were still in this area, and that this man is rightfully his prisoner! As the old man struggled to his knees, still pleading, I knew that taking this poor, crippled old man would put us dangerously behind the rest of the battalion which was still moving forward into the battle. We didn't have time to argue, so I quickly explained our falling behind, and told the raging GI that I was *ordering* him to leave the old man alone and move out!

In a flash, the GI whirled and aimed his M-16 right at my face! I was shocked to be looking at a distorted face of rage! He quickly glanced to confirm our aloneness, and then growled, from a tight throat, "You have just bossed your last nigger, *Honky!*" And then, "Oh, how I'm going to enjoy killing your ass, and no one will ever know where the bullet came from, you white motherfucker!"

Lucky for me, Strike got so caught up in venting his horrible rage, that he continued to expound on a racial litany of "*honky* injustices against his black brothers" and spewing it with such an apparent psychotic delight that a critical amount of time passed before he finally attempted to pull the trigger! Before he could do so, we heard voices ring out from the direction of our battalion. It was three of my men, thirty to forty yards away, each with their M-16s aimed at the momentarily deranged GI!!!

"Drop it, Strike!" they commanded! Strike flashed a surprised quick side glance at them, but kept his glare and aim on me, overcome by hate and rage! "I can get him and some of you too!" he yelled!

I then spoke to Strike in a calm, low voice, "Come on, Strike...we're falling behind; the old man's no threat. Let's get out of here." I was very careful not to make the slightest move or statement that might incite him to start blasting away! Terrifyingly, Strike still was not wanting to "let it pass." He certainly knew that he was in a shitty situation—whether from bullets or from legal consequences—and he didn't want to accept *either* outcome! An extremely tense couple of seconds passed, until one of my men said, "You don't want to die here, Strike, *none* of us do! Just think... you'd never get to go back to "*the world*" and screw beautiful women! Come on, man, lower your weapon."

At last Strike's eyes softened from their crazy rage. My squadmate's clever comment about Strike's *going back to America* seemed to be the magic words. Strike lowered his rifle and smiled broadly...as if this all was merely *a bad misunderstanding* or something. "I'm cool" (calm), he loudly called in a singsong tone to my men! Strike lowered his rifle barrel all the way and walked away in the direction of the battalion, casually singing some "Soul song" in his usual falsetto voice as he went. I started breathing again!

Had it not been for one of my men happening to see Strike aiming his M-16 at me and then quickly calling two nearby squadmates back, that day would have been my last one! As it turned out, after the battle, Strike was taken away in a helicopter by MP's! A day later, a platoon-mate flew in from our base camp where Strike had been taken to face a court martial. That platoonmate told us that Strike had tried to kill another guy while under *base-arrest,* but someone else knocked Strike out before he could kill his (also white) victim! Strike was a young man with an extremely sick, dark heart. He likely was court-martialed and spent the rest of his military time in jail. When "Strike" was eventually released from the Army, if he wasn't able to overcome his extreme racial bitterness, the young man probably committed more criminal acts and wasted most of his life behind bars somewhere in America. I wonder if he's still alive, or still in a jail.

Other War Crimes

Other war crimes witnessed involved harms against Vietnamese combatants and civilians. The first of these happened in my first deadly week with Charlie Company.

The K-Bar

My company had just been in a big battle in which five more of our men were killed. In that battle, we had captured an NVA colonel. Such a high-ranking enemy officer *surely* possessed valuable information!

Prior to the enemy's colonel being flown back to be interrogated by U.S. intelligence officials, he ended up on the ground in a small clearing in the wet jungle—with an extremely hard-core sergeant straddling his chest. The sergeant had his razor-sharp K-bar knife held to the colonel's throat and was interrogating him in Vietnamese while gripping the colonel's hair with his left hand. I walked into that clearing as this was happening. A group of six or so other GI's stood in a close circle around the spectacle on the ground in front of them.

We all watched intently as the colonel on the ground looked up with very cool eyes locked onto the sergeant's and said *nothing*...barely a blink out of him! After a few minutes of this interrogation being met with nothing but *stone silence,* the sergeant suddenly pressed the K-bar down and slashed all the way across the colonel's throat! Every GI spectator yelped in shock! One of them danced around in a tight circle of shock and revulsion after blood squirted onto his pant legs! "Jesus!!!" he nervously giggled in shocked disgust. *"Jesus H. Christ!!!"*

We were all absolutely wide-eyed and aghast...except for that sergeant, who stoically held tight to the now struggling enemy officer until the blood had stopped spurting and the colonel finally lay still. I wanted to look away but I couldn't! The sergeant then calmly wiped his bloody blade across the colonel's uniform, stood up and walked away without looking back. I remember nothing else about that scene. My mind went numb at that moment. I don't remember whether this happened before or after Shorty's tragic booby trap, but I do know that the deaths of five more of our men in this battle and Shorty's booby trap happened within days of each other. Rage was high, and human decency was low.

Already, my mind had been leaving the planet of my youth. I didn't know where in the universe I was right then, but I was no longer on earth. I think it might have been Hell.

Chieu Hoi

Another captive, at a different time, also had a bad ending. This combatant got caught out in the open one sunny afternoon as the front end of my platoon was traveling over a brushy hill. I was the fifth man from the front when I heard our point man yell, "Dung Lai!" "Dung Lai!"

We first five guys were the only ones to have crested the hill and were able to see the Cong. The Cong, rifle in hand, took off running! We raced off in hot pursuit, all of us sprinting through the low bushes with reckless abandon! In less than a minute, I heard a rifle shot coming from near the bottom of that hill's left side! In a few seconds, four of our five men caught up to our very hard-core point man who was standing and aiming his rifle down at the wounded Viet Cong soldier whom he had shot. Panting from our chase, we gathered around the Cong. We were the only members of our Point Platoon to arrive at the scene.

"Chieu Hoi," pleaded the Cong with a forced smile! A Chieu Hoi was an enemy who *turncoated over to the Allied side* after being captured. Our point man who shot him doubted the sincerity of the fallen Viet Cong! The Cong held his hand outward, between his face and the muzzle of the rifle that was aimed at him from three feet away. The point man coldly declared, "We don't take Chieu Hoi," and fired a full-automatic burst through the out-stretched hand, and continued shooting up and down the huddled torso and head! The result was as if a razor-sharp sword had completely sliced open the man! It was the first time I ever saw human brains.

Then the dispassionate point man/shooter turned and trotted away. Following his lead, we all trotted back to our platoon that we had left behind during our wild chase. All the way back, the only thing my mind could see was the *graphic image* of the Cong's violent demise *burnt* into my mind (I can *still* see it)! I don't remember (at the time) if I had thought about whether or not what had just happened was a crime or not. Of course, it was a crime according to the Geneva Convention; I just remember thinking how shitty war is!

The Female Farmer

Next, is a heartless APC commander shooting an unsuspecting female farmer! She was peacefully working in her rice paddy about 1,000 yards away. Though the distance to her was great, the tank commander's streams of .50 caliber tracer rounds verified his doubtlessly fatal hit! I and some other infantrymen who were near the APC, voiced our shocked protest even though he had the rank of captain! He just laughingly answered that he needed "target practice" before our upcoming battle! As his APC then rumbled away, he fixed us with a hard glare that clearly communicated, "Don't you lowly bastards *ever* speak to an *officer* in that tone again...and keep your damn mouths shut about this!"

As a side note, it was that same APC commander whose APC was later destroyed by the enemy rocket that sprayed me with shrapnel in the Battle Of Tam Ky. Both of us wounded, we were both flown out of battle on the same Medevac that night. He also ended up in the same MASH *after-surgery* recovery tent as me. His wounds to his legs were serious.

Though he was maimed for life, I'll always remember him sitting up in a bed across from me the next morning. All of us had been treated with potent painkillers, and the wounded captain clasped his hands casually behind his head and smiled broadly at us. Laughingly, he taunted us, "I'm going to be safely back in the good old U.S.A. in a few days, and you miserable bastards are going to be back out there getting your asses shot off!" The heartless man was a disgusting excuse of a human being.

A Not So Friendly Hug

I saw several other war crimes, but I will tell one more that affected me deeply and personally. It was by our battalion chaplain...a priest!

Earlier, this priest helicoptered out to our jungle clearing one Easter to say Mass for us. He was so drunk that he could barely stand up at the altar. My having been a devout Catholic altar boy while in school, I was one of two men serving mass for him at that service. I spent much of my time during that Easter Mass readying myself to catch him if he were to fall down! I was appalled, but my long-ingrained need to show respect for clergy compelled me try to withhold judgement.

The Chaplain's "worst self" came out sometime later though! My 2/1 Battalion's field base camp was an artillery firebase called LZ Ross. I had always felt lucky that my base camp, LZ Ross, was one that had a beautiful, warm stream flowing just outside its concertina wire perimeter. Best of all, the stream widened and slowed into an approximately 100′ x 70′ x 5′ deep pool. When off duty at the camp, we GI's were always eager to go down there! Since bathing suits were not part of our infantry pack items, and infantrymen didn't wear undershorts because of jungle rot danger, we just stripped down to nothing and enjoyed bathing, swimming, and playing water-football.

When not doing any of those three things, guys would just stand around in the chest-deep water and talk. This is when I encountered the worst side of our Chaplain who happened to be joining us in the stream one day. After a while, he motioned me over to where he was standing alone in chest-deep water under some overhanging bushes. We commenced in mundane, jovial talk. After a while, he suddenly pulled me close to him in a hug...and I was aghast to feel his erect penis pushed against my abdomen! I instantly felt shock, disgust, and outrage, and I quickly tried to push myself away but his big arms held tight. "Father!" I protested quietly but very strongly, "Let me go!" (Any other guy pulling that shit on me would have gotten a flurry of fists in his face, but the priest's "holy status" prevented me from doing that)!

I repeated myself even more strongly, but he just brushed it off with a calm whisper, "It's okay, it's okay...no one can see below the water over here." I warned him one more time, my eyes flashing with anger! Finally reading my eyes accurately, he backed away and replied with a *fake* smile, "Don't get excited...relax, relax! It was only a friendly hug."

"Friendly hug?" Bullshit to that! It was sexual assault by someone who was supposed to be my spiritual lifeline in that deadly war! I didn't report his serious misconduct; I now see that I should have. I just buried it away like many scared and intimidated victims sometimes do. I never attended any of his Masses again, and I soon disavowed my Catholic faith entirely! My faith had always been an important solace for me! It was *obliterated* in a few seconds by his actions!

Whatever anyone's attitude is about war, sexual orientation, religion, or priests, what happened to me there at LZ Ross was a *serious* violation and crime! It still creates much anger in me whenever I remember it!

War crimes! What sorrow, rage, guilt, and damage they create for the human spirit!

CS GAS IS NO LAUGHING MATTER

ONE OF THE NASTIEST TRAINING LESSONS that we experienced was being taught about CS gas. CS gas is "tear gas on *steroids!*" The purpose of this training was to prepare us for the possibility of getting exposed to it in Vietnam (which happened to me twice during the war). The *other* purpose of the training was to provide lowbrow humor for sadistic sergeants who gassed their trainees. I'm sure those sergeants had many hilarious stories at our expense!

There are three general areas for this training: (1) A designated place for us trainees to line up (which always filled me with great trepidation of what was in store); (2) A large tent into which *six-at-a-time* trainees would enter to be taught the wonders of CS gas, and; (3) Several fifty-five-gallon barrels out behind the torture tents...for the sole purpose of catching the breakfasts and lunches of the CS-educated trainees who burst out the tent's back door after their lesson.

It's not as much fun as it sounds. In fact, one might argue that a CS gas tent is what the Devil himself uses to punish some sinners for whom Hell is too *lenient!*

Here is my first-hand account of the CS lesson and its sadists (Err... I mean, *instructors*). First, while we stand stiff "at parade rest" in line anxiously awaiting our turn to enter the tent, we are treated to the sounds of extremely intense choking inside—much like what you might expect to hear at a *bronchitis farm.*

Then upon getting our turn, we double-time through an open tent flap that is swung back just long enough for us to enter into Hell. Inside, six gas-masked sergeants each take one of us to his smoking 55-gallon caldron of burning CS. Our eyes feel like someone has thrown hot battery acid into them! Of course, the sergeants know that each of us is cleverly holding his breath to spare his tender, pink lungs, so the sergeants demand that we trainee victims yell our name, rank, and serial number—the only three things that the Geneva Convention states that captured troops must declare to enemy captors. (Ironically, the Geneva Convention also outlaws use of tear gas...but then again, these sergeants weren't *technically* enemy captors).

Most of us still have some air left in our lungs after that, so we are cordially asked about our families, hobbies, and pets to force us to give up the last of our held breath. We hold out as long as humanly possible, but eventually we have to succumb to our lung's screaming demand to breathe! We opt to sneak "one tiny suck of air." Mistake! There is *no* good air in that tent...only CS gas! We begin to violently choke our fool heads off as our lungs are brutally assaulted by the horrible gas, which is not unlike vaporized lava!

While more lava enters our lungs, the comfortably gas-masked sergeants *continue* their friendly questions, "What are your life's goals? What kind of tree would you be if you were a tree?" By then our lungs have nearly been hacked right out of our chests, though some guys had prodigious lung capacity and *still* hadn't breathed any CS yet! Those guys were "complimented" by a sergeant sneaking up behind them and *whopping the hell* out of their ass with a large paddle!

The unfortunate downside of holding one's breath for a very long time is that the eventual inhale is deeper than a normal inhale! Soooooo: "GAAAASP! CHOKKKKKKKE! CHOKKKKKKKE! CHOKKKKKKKKKK-KE! One more tidbit of a CS gas lesson: CS is *highly* irritating to *all* mucus membranes! Not just the eyes and lungs, but also the nose, sinuses, and stomach! Tears and snot flowed like mountain streams down our face! And our stomachs *painfully* retched like they were filled with sharp nails and rotten snakes!

At that point, the sergeants, who don't want any vomit in their nice tent, open the rear tent flap and chase us out with their ass-whopping *paddles!* Entirely elated to finally be allowed to escape the CS Tent, we sprint into the tear-blurred daylight! Outside, we are quickly directed to *puke barrels* with a sergeant yelling, "DO NOT PUKE ON MY SOIL! TO THE DAMN BARRELS! QUICKLY…QUICKLY!!!" End of lesson. Next CS classroom: Vietnam.

CS in the Field—Story 1

My first experience with CS gas in the field was during a mission in which we were transported to a battle area, inside the protective steel walls of APC's (Armored Personnel Carriers). We disembarked into a flat region of dried-up rice paddies that were bordered by patches of thick hedgerows. An intense battle with a large NVA force ensued. The APCs' .50 caliber and .30 caliber machine guns blazed away along with our infantry M-16's, M-79 grenade launchers, and M-60 machine guns. Our weapons were answered by heavy barrages of enemy AK-47's, machine guns, and mortars!

At one point in the battle, my platoon was dashing from the cover of one hedgerow/paddy berm to the cover of another, briefly having to pass through an opening between the hedgerows. It was about a 100-foot dash without cover. Suddenly, streams of enemy machine gun tracers whizzed through that opening, coming from another hedgerow less than 100 yards to our right! I was halfway through—too far away from either hedgerow cover to safely go forward or back. I dove behind a tiny section of paddy dike, my only nearby cover! It was *barely* wide and high enough to shield me from the machine gun slugs that pelted my earthen cover and zinged by only an inch or two above my body! I flattened myself *tightly* to the ground!

Suddenly, to my horror, the air around me filled with a cloud of CS gas! My gas mask was in my backpack, but our packs were left inside the APC's for this assault! I couldn't breathe! I held my breath as long as I could then finally pressed my nose to the ground, hoping that the air down there was clean enough to breathe. There was too much gas down there, too! I was immediately choking my lungs out! Every attempt to inhale just allowed more CS gas to enter my lungs! My lungs seized shut! I was either going to succumb to suffocating or be pummeled with machine gun bullets if I rose to escape! My body was close to blacking out from lack of oxygen!

Suddenly, over the roar of the firefight going on around me, I heard a "hisssss" coming from beside me. Through heavy tears I could see that a jet of smoke was ejecting from my ammo belt! It was coming from *my* CS grenade which I had carried attached to my belt for weeks! A bullet had struck it! I immediately realized that I had only seconds to get rid of the CS before I passed out! With no safe space to reach back to detach it two-handed, I frantically tore at it with my right hand! My bullet-limited movement and my inability to see clearly made it so that I just couldn't detach it! My struggle to detach it used up all but the last 1% of my oxygen!

In desperation, I realized that my only hope of surviving was to unclasp my whole ammo belt with the damn CS grenade attached, and *fling* the ammo belt as far as I could! I flung it in the obvious direction of the machine gun fire, but from my prone position and with bullets flying close, the heavily laden belt probably only went about 20 feet! However, good fate had the air moving from me toward the gunner. Almost immediately I could gasp clean air! But I was still nearly overcome by the effects of taking in a *lot* of CS gas and not breathing for so long! Bullets whizzing 1 to 2 inches over my body now amazingly seemed like an acceptable threat!

In a few more seconds, the enemy gunner's machine gun *stopped!* I took a quick peek to evaluate then jerked my head back down. My peek revealed a CS cloud drifting over the hedgerow from where the enemy had been shooting. The gunner probably fled because of it! I looked toward the hedgerow cover from which I had dashed. Some of my platoon-mates were crouched there, and one was frantically motioning for me to get up and come back to where he was! It was a chance for me to escape my measly little island of protection that was perilously out in the open! I rose and dashed for my life! I made it safely and collapsed in a gasping, teary, mucus covered heap! A platoonmate poured some water from his canteen over my face. It helped only a little.

Very soon afterward, we got a command to pull back to the APC's. Still under the effects of CS poisoning, I was badly staggering as I reached an APC. A burly rear machine gunner reached down and iron-gripped my up-stretched arm and swung me atop the vehicle. I can't remember if I was still puking my guts out, but I probably was. I was a mental *mess* as the APC roared away.

I'd like to say that my ordeal ended as I steadily recovered and the battle ended, however, my damn CS-related ordeal wasn't done yet. That evening, I was told that the APC Battalion Commander wanted to see me...and that it wasn't a good thing! I'd never been in trouble before, but I was very apprehensive as I entered the field tent where he was waiting. Inside, a tall major was half-sitting on a table and glaring at me with a nasty sneer.

"Are you the soldier who abandoned his ammo belt, Private?!" I affirmed that I was, and offered what I thought would be received as a very understandable explanation of my life-or-death reason for doing so.

"I don't give God-damn *shit* about that," he yelled back! "A soldier *never* leaves his ammo belt on the battlefield for an enemy to find! There were hand grenades and full ammo clips on that belt which the enemy could have used to kill your fellow soldiers!" I tried to defend myself, "But, Sir, I was nearly unconscious and there were enemy machine gun bullets skimming my ass, and I had to..."

"At ease, Private!" he bellowed. "You're just damn lucky that one of our APC's found it when we swept through that area later! If it had turned out that the enemy found it before we did you'd be facing a damn *court-martial!*"

I felt *half* scared from being chewed out so hard by a major, but also felt *half* pissed that he refused to understand that my only alternative in that extraordinary circumstance was *suffocation!* "I'm very glad that it was recovered by one of our guys, Sir," I replied. "I'm also glad to get my own belt back because I have a real good camera in one of my belt's pouches!"

The officer gave me another sneering smile and said, "It was destroyed. It's gone." I could tell that he was lying and that *he* was probably the owner of my camera now! But to call an Army Major a liar, with or without having any proof that he wasn't telling the truth...shit! He had me!

The major then put on his best angry frown and stared me down. "You're dismissed, Private," he then said coldly with a clear tone of finality that suggested that if I opened my mouth again it would be at my own great peril.

"Thank you, Sir," I said as I saluted and left the tent. Lucky he couldn't hear my *mind* screaming, "Thank you...you pompous, thieving prick!"

CS in the Field—Story 2

My second experience with CS gas in the field was at the hands of the enemy! At that time, I had risen to the rank of sergeant and was a squad leader in the 11th Infantry Brigade. I had transferred to the 11th because our American Division had requested their infusion of combat experienced soldiers from my 196th Infantry Brigade. The entire 11th Brigade had shipped en masse from their base in Hawaii to Vietnam without any of them having been in combat! Transferees like me would be their critically needed "on-the-job teachers."

The day of the gassing had gone pretty normal up to that point. Our company was in the process of setting up camp for the night and our site was on a flat, open area above a small stream. A steep 30-foot high dirt bank separated us from the stream. Everyone had dug their foxholes up on the flat area. However, when scouting my squad's assigned area, I found an already-dug hole that appeared to be something that an enemy soldier might have excavated just below the top of the steep bank. This hole in the bank overlooked the stream; it was perfect shelter that provided great overhead protection plus great rifle-coverage of any attack from across the stream!

By late afternoon, we were chatting and getting ready to cook our C-ration dinners. Suddenly, from across the stream—about 150 yards into the forest—I heard the hollow sounds, "Poomp!" "Poomp!" "Poomp!" I recognized the sounds as *mortars* being fired—*and not our own!*

Alarmed, I looked across the flat camp at our men who were casually acting as if nothing was going on! I was shocked that they weren't dashing for their foxholes! However, with scant combat experience, they didn't recognize this imminent threat!

I quickly hollered, "Mortars* were just fired at us! They'll be hitting in a few seconds! Get to cover!!!" Confused men grabbed their helmets and rifles and ducked into their foxholes. I jumped into my bank-side hole and backed deep into it with M-16 ready! "The rounds were fired from across the stream," I added loudly.

Then, the sounds of "Thud-Snap!" "Thud-Snap!" "Thud-Snap!" I knew that those were the mortars hitting around our company's camp… but, sans the explosions! Their mortar rounds must be *duds,* I thought! More "Poomps!" sounded from across the stream.

Then one of the guys near the "Snapping" rounds yelled, "Gas… TEAR gas!" Immediately, I realized what was going on! The enemy was first dropping tear gas rounds to get GI's panicking and out of their cover to get their gas masks…then following with *exploding* shrapnel rounds to blast those above-ground GI's! It would be a blood bath for our unprotected men!

I thrust my head up above the bank and screamed back at my inexperienced mates, "Stay down! Stay down! There'll be shrapnel rounds coming behind the gas!" About three seconds later, a hail of explosions: BOOM! BOOM! BOOM! BOOM! I ducked to the back of my dirt cave as the rounds exploded around my company's camp! I prayed, "Man, I hope their foxholes are deep enough and nobody gets a *direct hit.*" As I watched for any enemy attacking from the other side of the stream, I suddenly heard a weird "throbbing buzz" getting louder and louder. Then, "Whump!" A foot-long, 3-lb chunk of shrapnel *chopped* into the excavated dirt mound in front of my cave inches in front of my face!

"SHIT," I hissed with shocked surprise! My eyes were surely as wide

---

* Mortars are bombs that are shot from ground-based metal tubes, making a hollow "Poomp!" sound when fired. Mortars arc hundreds of feet into the air after being fired and, seconds later, they come down and explode when they hit the ground, sending horrible shards of metal outward!

as saucers as I beheld the vicious looking, jagged edged chunk of metal in front of me. "That thing would have *chopped* my *arm off* if I had it extended out there," I exclaimed to myself! I was *very* impressed at how deadly the shrapnel appeared to be.

Then (because that's what boys do), I reached out to haul it in. Concerned about the shrapnel's razor-sharp edges, I clamped my fingers carefully around its flat sides to pull it out of the dirt. "YOW, I yelped to myself!" I had not counted on the chunk of metal still being nearly *red hot.* Even though it had twirled like a boomerang high into the air before thudding back to earth, it still had enough heat to blister my fingers. "Damn," I marveled, "these things will not only chop into a body like a heavy meat cleaver, they'll also burn the shit out of the poor victim too!"

I don't remember if any of our guys were killed or injured in that attack. PTSD has wrecked most of my war memory. I do intend to phone one particular member of my squad to see if he remembers those details. (This squadmate, John Bietzel, mentioned this gas attack in an e-mail correspondence to me a few years ago. John's emails showed that he has a *mind like a steel trap!* For sure he'll remember!).

At any rate, the strategic addition of my combat experience to this 11th Brigade Company most likely prevented injuries and deaths to my less experienced, *above-ground* soldiers! There is just no substitute for experience—especially in combat!

That was my second time being gassed in Vietnam. This time, though, I didn't receive even one little whiff of the enemy's CS gas because my bank-side cave was upwind from the CS mortar rounds. However, there's a great *irony* in my two CS encounters in Vietnam: this *enemy's* CS gas caused no harm to me, but my *own* CS grenade earlier very nearly got me killed!

THE COMBAT VETERAN RETURNS HOME

HAVING SERVED A MONTH AND A HALF "COMBAT EXTENSION" of my year in Vietnam, my Army obligation had been fulfilled. I got off my long flight back to Fort Lewis, Washington and immediately went through out-processing. Before issuing my ticket back to Montana, the Army's discharge sergeant explained the "decompressing" benefit of my remaining in the army for a few "readjustment days." I strongly declined! I wanted to be a free civilian again more than you could imagine! Subsequently, *only days* would pass between my helicoptering out of the jungle in Vietnam to sitting in the living room of my Great Falls home! In retrospect, I would not recommend that quick of a transition to any troop who had been in heavy combat! For weeks, my mind reeled at the bizarre juxtaposition of realities!

In my first days home, one of my buddies took me to a party where all of my pre-war friends were gathered just as they had always done since high school. Opening the door to the party room, my buddy loudly announced, "Hey everyone, look who I got!" I walked in to a chorus of, "Jewell! You're back! Wow, look at that tan!" They expressed gladness to see me back, and a cold beer was quickly handed to me with a few more comments about my dark tan. My tan was the only discussion of my having been in Vietnam. The party continued, the same as before I arrived. But I remember sitting there, looking around the room, *screaming inside my mind,* "How in the hell can you all be treating me as if I was the *same* Bob Jewell?! Don't you realize that I was *killing people* and fighting for my life just days ago?!!!"

My friends never did say a word about me being in the war—even years after that party. We talked about everything *except* that. I experienced the same thing at home with my family...*Nothing* about my combat. I learned, decades later, that changes in my face loudly broadcast that I had experienced major trauma! It turns out that everyone feared that my being in war was not a subject to be introduced. They didn't know what to say or how I'd react. Thus, without any discussion of my combat experiences, combat got buried, one heavy shovelful of dirt at a time.

That fall, eager to build a new life, I entered college at Montana State in Bozeman! I first lived with some high school friends from Great Falls. One of them, Tom Zadick, told me that waking me up in the morning "was an adventure." I'd wake-up wide-eyed and scary! On the outside, I was working hard to be a college student, but on the inside I was still an infantryman.

One sunny day, I came out of the MSU Student Union Building and beheld a loud angry crowd of war protesters. I was stunned by signs and angry rhetoric proclaiming that that Vietnam War soldiers were "criminals and baby killers!" Their furor made me feel certain that I would be viciously attacked if someone recognized me and yelled: *"Look, there's one of them!"*

My eyes darted around at faces in that crowd, fearfully looking for anyone who knew me and my horrible secret. I felt like a "criminal fugitive!" Many of my college memories for that first year involved feeling like an *outsider* for having been a "killer." I felt tainted. I wasn't one of those fresh-faced kids anymore. They surely would not have accepted me as one of their peers anymore. I kept my combat locked away inside...a deep dark secret!

For my first months before college, and during weekends of my first college year, I drank heavily with my pals at night. Occasionally, as before Vietnam, I would get into a "normal fistfight" outside one of my favorite bars. One evening, however, I got into it with the toughest guy I ever fought. He was a visitor from Anaconda, Montana—a town known for its tough guys. Soon into the fight, I realized that he was also an *insane* fighter—not just the usual "slug-it-out, then go back into the bar type!" His toughness and ferocity led me to believe that he intended to kill me, and my mind went into a dangerous life-or-death *combat mode!* My own fighting skills eventually allowed me to land a very hard punch to his nose that had him on his back, temporarily stunned. In my previous fights, the fight would have ended then—or at *least,* it would have continued only after I had waited for the guy to get up. However, this time my mind was in a blind, raging terror that he would surely kill me when he got up...so I pounced on him and started slamming his head against the parking lot pavement!

Quickly, the spectators—mostly his and my friends who had gathered around our fight, pulled me off the then unconscious fighter! My friends hustled me away from the crowd, saying that someone had called the cops! I was scuffed up and feeling some throbbing aches from the hard punches thrown as we drove away. But *mostly* I was feeling shock and dismay that I had been so out of control...that I tried to *murder* a man! I immediately saw that any future release of that uncontrolled rage could put me in *prison!* And prison would be too much like being locked away in combat in Vietnam again! *Then and there,* I firmly promised sobriety, no drugs, and strong positive thinking for the rest of my life! I have *kept* that vow.

Then, 18 years passed after combat. During that period I was in a state of incredible peace, joy, and productivity! I'd finished college and had become a passionate teacher and school counselor. My life seemed *perfect* during that time! My subconscious mind had buried the bad stuff and allowed only extremely whitewashed memories of Vietnam. "Vietnam seemed pretty boring." Then the Walls of Jericho came tumbling down!

That tumble started during the first week of graduate school—after entering the Masters program at MSU in 1987. There, a Pandora's Box briefly opened in a "practice counseling session" (described earlier in these Vietnam War memoirs in my "Two Hearts Racing" chapter). I managed to temporarily re-cage Pandora. But she would *fully* awaken six years later, in 1995, after an extremely traumatic and exhausting investigation and trial of a heartless man who had murdered my dear, sweet youngest brother.

Awake this time, Pandora *savaged* my mind with vicious rabid bites—bites known by their clinical term as Post-Traumatic Stress Disorder (PTSD). The trauma of dealing with that murder, plus two other large stressors, resurrected ugly Pandora with a wild vengeance! Pandora completely flooded my mind with graphic, *horrifically* violent 24-hour images of me *fiercely* defending myself, family, friends, and fellow students from an *endless* onslaught of imagined attackers! No matter how hard I tried to shut out the intrusive images, they persisted mercilessly. The onslaught had no end! Somehow, I endured five straight months of continually violent and near sleepless nights! My only "sleep" during all of that time consisted of two to three hours of *unimaginably violent* nightmares! I still don't know how I survived that horrible period without sustaining total collapse!

Medication and minimal therapy from the nearby Fort Harrison Veterans Hospital eventually eliminated 99 percent of the violent ideation and returned some of my functioning. Nevertheless, the psychological damages of PTSD ravaged my strength and diminished the last years of my career in education. Very sadly, it forced me to retire during a time in which I still possessed the passion to contribute to the care and education of our youth. I look back at that ending with a heaviness in my heart because I had experienced so many extraordinarily joyful and productive years as a teacher and counselor prior to the onset of PTSD.

After retirement, I was finally free to devote full time to my PTSD which had gone into a rapid and dangerous tailspin! My VA-contracted therapist up in Great Falls got me quickly accepted into an extraordinary 6-week in-patient PTSD program at the Boise, Idaho Veterans Hospital. I truly owe my life to their talented VA staff! There, they skillfully helped me to expose Pandora instead of "re-boxing" her, and strengthened me enough to be *tougher* than her! My worst fear had always been that Pandora was powerful enough to "take me over the cliff" if she ever got out of her box! Though mental challenges still arise, I no longer live at the edge of that cliff.

Since Boise, I've continued to de-clutter my mind by writing about my war experiences, dredging up repressed secrets from the depths so that I can reconcile them. Additionally, it seems useful for me to document powerful war events and feelings so that people may gain further valuable insights into the story of current or planned wars. I experienced many things in combat that seem too important to leave unwritten. Unwritten, they vanish forever like wisps of smoke.

The value of one of my writings, the poem "Two Hearts Racing," was demonstrated by a famous author, Stephen Ambrose (author of *Band Of Brothers, Citizen Soldier, Undaunted Courage, Eisenhower*). Mr. Ambrose was writing a new book about the Vietnam War: how it affected *all of America* (the veterans, their family and friends, the war protesters, the police, and politicians, etc.). He advertised for Americans to submit their personal Vietnam War stories for him to consider for inclusion in his book. My fiancee read Mr. Ambrose's advertisement and wanted me to submit my poem! I resisted, but gave her the o.k. to send him my poem anyway. Weeks later, I received a letter from Mr. Ambrose saying, "Your poem is exactly what I was looking for! I would like to use it in my book with your written permission." Appreciatively, I signed my name on the permission line of his letter and mailed it back to him. Unfortunately, Stephen Ambrose died of cancer about a year later, and his book never reached completion. Nevertheless, his interest in my poem reinforced my belief that there's value in people writing about their traumatic experiences.

My literary journey from Vietnam to the present has been long and difficult…and painful. To my deep frustration, important memories still remain hidden despite my sincere willingness to confront them. I'm truly amazed at how tenaciously my worst war memories resist the slightest exposure to air! As such, much of my peace of mind now comes more from simply accepting that "shit happens" than from being able to process every single memory.

After-Effects of Combat

There are so many things a person can lose in combat! Terrible losses include genitals, hearing, legs, arms, face, or mind. None of my disabilities are complete losses, thank the Lord. My bullet and shrapnel scars have mostly faded. However, I still get occasional flare-ups on my hip from the grenade shrapnel wounds. Some of them become bright red and produce an extremely fierce itch that is only quelled by applying hydrocortisone cream!

I believe that in many ways, combat forged me into a better person than I would have been otherwise. My life is a multi-faceted treasure...an important focus that I have consciously nurtured to maintain!

This is the final chapter on my "list of events to document." Many other important experiences in Vietnam are lost to repression, but at least I retrieved these. They were written over a span of nearly two decades. Writing some of the chapters caused me to stop breathing at times, lose sleep, have strong anxiety attacks, and left me emotionally drained on days after penning them. However, I *needed* to get them out of my head and onto paper! *Bleeding Spirits* has been a great catharsis. Importantly, I also need to emphasize that I couldn't have *safely* attempted these memoirs if I had not previously gone through the Boise VA Hospital's 6-week in-patient PTSD therapy program! That therapy gave me the vital tools to write this with a safe mind.

I just now gave a huge sigh at the realization that I don't have to document any more. I'm done. The End! I can now allow my mind to rest more easily. Amen to rest.

February 28, 2017

About the Author

Robert E. Jewell

ROBERT "BOB" ELLSWORTH JEWELL was a true Montana man who valued family, friends, the arts, education, precision, hard work, philosophy, and having fun. Aside from his time serving in the United States Army, he lived his entire life in Montana. He was born in Great Falls and spent most of his life in Helena. The Montana mountains and rivers were his sanctuary and he passionately lived his life trying to preserve mother nature. The roles Bob played in his life were what he cherished most. He was a beloved father to Sheri Erhardt and Holly Pozzi, a "boppa" (grandpa) to five grandchildren, a brother to four siblings, a cousin, an uncle, a friend, a teacher, a counselor, and a squad leader. Bob was truly treasured and respected for his gracious kindness, witty sense of humor, passionate storytelling, intelligence, and loving spirit.

Most of his time growing up in Great Falls, Montana was spent outdoors in parks, fishing the Missouri river, playing sports, seeking out treasures, and getting into a little (or a lot) of mischief. His family didn't have a lot of money, yet happily lived a simple life. Bob had a close network of friends while growing up whom he uniquely remained connected with throughout his entire life. Bob always took great pride in his work ethic and extreme precision in his work, which likely was a character trait that kept him and his squad members alive in the Vietnam War. As soon as he was old enough, he worked at a smelter and in highway construction before being drafted into the United States Army to serve in the Vietnam war in 1967. He was assigned to the Americal Division with the Charlie Company 2/1 of the 196th Light Infantry Brigade and later with the Delta Company of the Divisions 4th/21. His 416 days he served in the Vietnam war were life-altering in many ways. His mother later said that the son that left for Vietnam never really returned.

Upon returning from the war, Bob went to college at Montana State University where he earned a bachelor's degree in Education, and several years later a master's degree in School Counseling. He was a celebrated Earth Science teacher and school counselor for nearly 30 years in the Helena schools. His animated lessons and mindful counseling passionately delivered the message to his students to preserve and appreciate Mother Earth, be kind and understanding of others, laugh often and deeply, be a life-long learner, do your own research, and leave the world a better place than you found it.

While attending Montana State University, Bob fell in love and married Cynthia in 1971. They were married for 18 years and had two daughters together. Bob and Cynthia put great care and love into raising their girls, making certain they instilled what they felt were the most important values in life: be generous with your love and kindness, appreciate what you have, put time into everything you do so it is done well, discover and develop your innate abilities, be honest, be considerate of others regardless of how they treat you, and family and good friends are most important. Throughout Bob's life, he had a wealth of friends and family that shared a deep love and adoration with him.

Bob was a unique, creative, patient, compassionate, inspiring human being with a gentle spirit. Beyond being a fabulous educator and loving person to many, he was also an artist and the world was his canvas. His every move was an art form, done with extreme precision and care. He had an eye for seeing the beauty in people and in the simple things in life. Although his experiences in Vietnam and subsequent PTSD haunted him and influenced his ability to lead the life he intended, he did his absolute best to create beautiful relationships and leave the world a better place. The sparkle of love in his eyes while in his company revealed his genuine character. With his laughter, kind words, tender care, you knew you were treasured. Bob passed away in December 2017 after a battle with Mesothelioma. He was still putting his final edits on this book in the last weeks of his life. This book was probably one of his greatest challenges, yet also was therapeutic for him. Although a profuse researcher, he was not a reader of books, adding to his challenge of writing his own book. Aside from his enduring love with his family and friends, this book is his final gift he left behind.

REMEMBRANCES

Note from Tom Gannon

Lifelong friend of Robert Jewell

BOB JEWELL AND I GREW UP ON THE SAME STREET, 7th Avenue, on the north side of the city of Great Falls, Montana. My family owned a small cattle ranch southwest of town where I spent most of my time. We went to the nearby Saint Gerard Catholic grade school together, on 5th Avenue, then to Central Catholic High School, and spent a little time at the Catholic College of Great Falls. Bob ran out of money, and I ran out of "school endurance," both of us dropping out and getting drafted into the U.S. Army. Both of us were sent to Vietnam after four to five months of Basic and Advanced Training. His tour started early 1968, the very bloodiest year!

I arrived late 1968 in Vietnam as a Military Policeman, thereby avoiding actual combat. The 1st Infantry Division Headquarters (Big Red One) was about eighty miles North of Saigon at Lai Khe. We suffered rocket attacks on an irregular interval the whole time I was there through January 6, 1970. As an MP, I had various assignments: guard duty to Division Headquarters and guarding the General's personal helicopter. One of the 1st Infantry's commanding Generals was shot down and killed while out on a mission. I helped escort medical doctors to outlying villages, guarding the area while they attended to civilian medical needs. I also helped investigate a suspicious death of a soldier at a northern remote firebase that lead to my first helicopter ride. I was a Colonel's driver for 5 months, keeping his Jeep dust free and shining, which was about half of the boring job. Not knowing it at the time, high ranking officers were highly prized targets for the Viet Cong, but I thought it was a "safe" job. No jobs were safe. Clerks, cooks, Colonel's drivers all suffered casualties.

But, I will end any comparison of my experiences to the front line "grunts," the U.S. Army Infantry Soldiers who faced direct combat with the enemy. The danger and fear they faced were terrifying. Many people are not able to read what Bob Jewell wrote due to the graphic description of what he experienced. It may be tough reading, especially for Vietnam Veterans who may have experienced similar instances. But his memoir is important. I invite you to start reading reviews starting on the very last page by Sandy Casey who was a coworker of Bob's for years in Helena. The next review is a letter to me on the next to last page from Bob Brown, a lawyer friend of mine from Butte. He wrote a very well-crafted review of *Bleeding Spirits*. Then, Bob Jewell's introduction: "Caution Before Reading," and then the first chapter, "My Entering the War: The Effect on my Family."

I experienced many of the same effects Bob has documented. Finally, proceed with caution. I have read and re-read *Bleeding Spirits* and have been brought to tears every time. If you struggle to read his memories, I understand. Pass the book on.

Thank you,

Tom

February 6, 2018

Comments from Bob Brown

Friend of Tom Gannon

Tom,

As I do not know how to contact Mr. Jewell nor do I know whether any contact would be appreciated, I am emailing you, Tom, and will defer to your judgment whether to forward/share my email with Mr. Jewell.

Having just finished the last page of Mr. Jewell's memoir, I am sitting here stunned and touched by his courage and generosity in writing *Bleeding Spirits*. Vietnam scarred America's psyche as much as any other event in my lifetime. That Mr. Jewell has shared such a poignant, personal, and quintessential story of his Vietnam and post-Vietnam life experiences is a selfless act of inspirational grace. What a blessing he had to have been to his students while teaching and serving as a guidance counselor.

But even more important, what an unequivocal gift his memoirs are to those of us who were alive and coming of age in the 1960's and 70's who have striven to make sense of the impact of the Vietnam War on our America and the world. Not since reading Philip Caputo's *A Rumor of War* have I had more cogent exposure to what the War meant to the very real people who through no choice of their own had to fight the war. While Ken Burns' Vietnam movie which recently was telecast on PBS over a two-week period presented a macro overview of the Vietnam War, Mr. Jewell's first-person micro account of real events he witnessed is even more impactful.

Growing up in northeastern Montana (I graduated from high school in 1970—my draft number was 362), my understanding of what had happened and was happening in the Vietnam War was primarily via television reporting. My WWII Marine father never talked with us regarding his service as a "grunt" (his word, not mine) in the Pacific Theater other than to disparage the Vietnam antiwar protesters as being cowards—only he usually used stronger, more profane, terms. Our high school history teacher never talked about the Vietnam War. When Robert Brown (from Park Grove, Montana who had graduated from Nashua High School in 1965) died I believe 1968 in Vietnam, no one where I grew up ever really talked about the War like Mr. Jewell has.

Further, not until I was attending the University of Montana Law School in 1979 did I have a close friend who had served in Vietnam, and only then did I begin to comprehend, at least a little, what the Vietnam War had meant to many of my generation and enormous sacrifice America had imposed upon a small percentage of Americans. Reading Mr. Jewell's memoir, particularly regarding how the War was viscerally ingrained into his very being, has given me even greater respect for those who served America in the face of the political machinations in Washington, D.C.

I wish I would have been one of his students. His two daughters must be so proud he is their father. Please convey my gratitude to Mr. Jewell for his profoundly courageous gift. My hope is that his memoir will be published as it is a true story which must be read widely if we hope to learn from his hard-won wisdom and his enormous sacrifice.

Bob Brown

A Letter to Robert Jewell from Sandy Casey

Teaching colleague, Helena High School

Bob,

Since I wasn't sure when our paths would cross again, I thought perhaps I would share my reflections about *Bleeding Spirts* this way. However, as I tried to compose this note to you, I found it took several attempts to get my thoughts on paper. You gave me a lot to think about.

First, thank you so much for having the courage to share your incredible story of survival and resilience with Ron and also with me. We both read your manuscript within a couple of days (passed it on to Tucker and Anne). Because of his own Vietnam experiences, I am sure Ron related to your stories much differently than I did. For me I felt honored that you let me read it. I found it to be a compelling read, a powerful narrative that took me on a very emotional journey. One that pulled me from intense, heart-racing fear to out-loud laughter; from a deep sorrow to a quiet peace knowing that you have found solace through your writing. As I read, I also tried to reconcile the horrific experiences described on the pages with my recollection of the quiet, gentle, caring teacher with whom I had worked and of the person I know today.

Your collection of stories also caused me to pause in order to reflect on war and its impact on a nation, on a generation, on families and in particular, on the individuals who are asked to serve. Since Vietnam, America has been engaged in a series of battles, to the point where it seems to be an unending war. It has been years of deployments, fighting, near-death experiences and the loss of life. Sadly, as a society,

I believe we have become desensitized to or worse yet, chosen to ignore these atrocities. Your story reminded me that war is not an abstract concept. Through your writing, you asked me to internalize the "real" consequences of world leaders who decide to engage in war for reasons such as political power, territorial acquisition, religious separatism or commercial gain. I found myself asking…what happened to our moral compass?

Bleeding Spirits definitely made an impression. Thank you so much for sharing. I admire your internal strength and your quiet spirit. You are a brave fighter and a very gifted writer.

Peace,

Sandy

P.S. I think I told you that Barb Holliday and I have remained friends over the last 40 years. She had recommended I watch *Arrival*. So I told her we had watched it at your home and that we had the great discussion following the movie. She sent an email, the end of which included this: "…If you see Bob Jewell, please tell him two things from me. I loved him as a science teacher at middle school, and recall fondly a field trip where we went to test water from a stream and viewed all the mysterious microbial life in it. It is a clear and good memory."

CORRESPONDENCE

Letters Home

29 Aug 68

Dear All,

Here is just a note to explain my change of address. I have been infused to the 11th Inf. Bde. The reason — remember that I came over here in a large packet of men? Well we are all going home at the same time, and if we weren't infused out of the Brigade, there would be too large a change-over. You can see how everyone going home at once would not be good, can't you?

So about sixty guys, who came over in February, are being infused from each battalion in the 196th Brigade — and

-over-

I was one of the fortunate (?) men on the list.

Of course, the are both the "pros" and the "cons" of this infusion for me. First of all, the 196th did most of the fighting in Americal Division. The 11th Bde does a little combat (comparatively) but, on the average, has less dangerous missions than the 196th. The battalions of the 11th are here and there between Duc Pho and Da Nang. One battalion is around Chu Lai, and another is at L.Z. "Baldy" (where Cutler is.) I will be in the 4th/21st battalion, but I don't know if that is one of the two I just mentioned. I'll find out later.

Also good about this infusion is that all the paper-work involved takes about a week. So during this time, I am spending lots of time on the beach and at the clubs here at Chu Lai. — Vacations are nice, once in a while.

What's bad about the infusion is this: I was taken out of an E-5 sergeant's slot (rifle team-leader) and will no doubt be dropped into a P.F.C. slot (rifle-man.) I've got my corporal rank already but I'll still be doing a PFC's job at first. And, being a new man in that company, it will take a long time to work my way back up to team-leader... unless the leaders in my new squad are noticeably less sharp than myself. But, the

over-way it looks now, I may not even make sergeant.

Also, I had to leave all of my good friends in the 196th. A lot of great guys they were too! I know I would have had to leave them sooner or later, but I would have liked to have worked with them as long as possible. We worked together great and definitely ~~knew~~ how to team up on the gooks. So you can see why I'm not too enthusiastic about being infused out of one of the best units over here.

Man! I just got some crushing news from my "old" company. The day I left "C" company to be infused, one of my very best friends in my squad hit an enemy booby trap with a 60mm explosive

charge attached to it. It
blew both of his hands off,
filled his body full of holes,
and blew his eyes out. I
couldn't believe it. No one
can imagine how bad I felt
when I heard that. I couldn't
ask for a better friend than
Shorty. I think I would have
given my life to prevent
what happened to him. But
now that it's done, all I
can do is pray the God has
mercy on what is left of him,
and gives Shorty the tremendous
strength needed to take such
a mishap. At the present,
Shorty wishes he were dead...
how can anyone blame
him?!!
    Well, I guess I'll close
                    -over-

now and mail this right
away so you can write me
soon. Here is my new
address:

Sp/4 Bob Jewell US56638219
"D" 4/21 11th Inf. Bde.
APO S.F. 96217

I will write to all my
friends and relatives as soon
as I can, but if you see
them before, why don't you
tell them my new address?
Okay?!! So until later...

With Love,
Bob

P.S. Bill, school will be just
about starting when you all
get this letter. Please do me
a great favor: Start off well, study
hard, and make this year a "breeze."
TRY?

21 OCT 68

Dear Eve, George, & Kids,

Hi. Received your letter a couple of days ago. I'm glad to hear everyone is well there, especially Sonny. It's a good thing he's tough. As for myself, I'm fine now – wounds all healed up. After a month out of action, I'm finally back playing combat.

Our company is operating in a different type of terrain than what I've seen. The entire area is a close "checkerboard" of white sand dikes. The dikes are about 4 to 10 feet high and have rows of oriental pines growing on top of them. This provides great cover and consealment for the V.C. in their close-combat tactics. Snipers are everywhere.

—OVER—

Consequently, the area is named "Sniper Valley." One such sniper "hosed us down" last evening with a light-machine-gun. Didn't hit anyone, but the lead was sure flying! They never let us see themselves and are long gone before we can maneuver on them. We have to really be on our toes, watching for those S.O.B.'s.

So you want to hear my views on the Viet Nam situation, huh? Okay then, I'll sock it to ya. Here it is —

First of all, my life (while I am here) depends on my being able to kill _first_. This is why I, as well as the military in general, may have "hawk" views. However, being a real indivirdualist, a few "dove" notes may seep into my views still.

I can see the effects of

Communist force against the people of South VietNam. These people _do_ hate the V.C., and would do a "helluva" lot more to drive them out—if it were not for one thing. That one thing is that the GI's make such a nuisance of themselves to the civilians, that the people have a hard time deciding which is the worst — us or the V.C. When "G.I. Joe" comes through a village and burns, steals, or destroys their property, kills their farm-animals, kicks the old people around, and sometimes rapes a girl, then are we to expect them not to turn V.C.? But they do turn V.C., and in this Northern part of South Vietnam about 75% of the population is

—OVER—

active V.C. or "V.C. - sympathetic".
I think the GI's behavior, <u>not</u>
American policy, is what has
lost (already) this war <u>socially</u>.
Militarily, we are kicking ass!
In other words, we are winning
their battles—but losing their <u>hearts</u>.
So thusly we are defeating our
purpose because making these
people like our way is what
really counts.

30 OCT 68

We can leave Vietnam only
when the South Viets can fight (win)
their own battles. If we were
to leave right now, however, South
Vietnam would be Communist
controlled in a matter of days.
This is because the South Viet Army
is not nearly strong or big enough
to win, also because the
civilian population probably
wouldn't contribute support to
the cause. We screwed up by

trying to win their hearts. Govt. to govt. we may have attempted that, but not person to person (G.I. to Vietnamese.) An extreme clash of personalities between the two is to blame for that. It's hard for most GI's to show friendliness to people who he feels are responsible for his being in this war. The G.I. also sees these people almost as animals because of their uncivilized and begging ways. Also, any one of these "friendly" gooks, today, may be our killer tomorrow. So you can see our point too!

I myself, am one of the few GI's who treat the Vietnamese friendly. I can see their point of view too and I prefer to judge them as individuals. If all of

—OVER—

my soldier buddies could be like that, we would score a great victory. Then all we would have to worry about would be the infiltrating army of Ho Chi Mink's regulars.

In summary to my long-winded gab-session, I would like to say this on <u>behalf</u> of nearly <u>every</u> soldier in Viet Nam: This war is very frustrating in that the end isn't foreseeable, but the purpose is to prevent Communism from robbing our children and grandchildren of the freedoms of democracy which we enjoy today. And for that cause we are proud, <u>damned</u> proud, to be a part of... even at cost of life.

And no American in Viet Nam appreciates the anti-war demonstrators' "contribution" to their national heritage. We wonder if all the REAL Americans are there or <u>here</u>.

I'll tell you though; with each returning soldier from Viet Nam, the U.S. is one American stronger. I will showing my "colors" when I return.

Well I hope you get the picture now. Its really difficult to put "my views" into words well because my mind is so con-gested with feelings about my (our) being here. But anyhow there it is, the best I could do on it.

And do you notice how long it took me to to finally complete this letter. Between snipers and ambushes, I had a hard time staying at it. But I'd better send it off now before something else comes up to delay it. Hope this letter finds everyone "tip-top" and smiling. So long now

Much Love Bob

30 OCT 68

Dear Clay & Nancy,

  Well, believe it or not, I finally got time to write back to you. Sorry for not writing sooner, but the gooks have been keeping our minds on pieces of lead rather than letters.

  I got out of the hospital on about October sixth and then was kept out of action 'til a month after I got hit. I was sure thankful for the long break. My wounds had _enough_ trouble staying closed even as I was taking it easy in the _rear_. The scars are shrinking a lot and should be small and light by the time I get back to "the world."

  Upon returning to action

my company was just headed into an area named "Sniper Valley" (appropriately named too.) The first day out, the gooks shot down a plane nearby, and we had to go to the rescue. We found the plane burning and exploding, having been crashed into a mountainside. The pilot was dead, cooked in fact, and we had to pull him out in pieces. Sure was a sorry scene.

But after that was taken care of, we had to head into the heart of Sniper Valley. The mission — to bring for trial, a <u>12</u> year old girl (Viet) who had been raped by two lousy "shit-birds" from our company. It was an absurd case. Two horny G.I.'s (one a <u>dud lieutenant</u>) ~~they~~ had pulled that off during the month before when we were there. This was the first rape case I have seen in Nam — I hope it's the last. A court-martial is too good for them. So into that valley we went to bring the girl back. That may have cost one man his life and many of the rest of us were almost hit (including me.) The kid who did get hit had only been in action for eight days. Snipers were everywhere and we never could even see them. I never want to see that valley again. It's bad shit!

Hey I never have got that "A-1" sauce yet. I sure hope it gets here. These "C"'s are getting funky. I got a big package from Mom yesterday.

— OVER —

I couldn't have asked for better contents. She sent some instant soup mix that is <u>ideal</u> in these monsoons.

I'm looking forward to the family's big visit out there next summer. That should be a lot of fun. It will be great to see you all again Better be in practice on the "greens", Clay. I'll be able to get in shape all spring before the visit. You two will probably have your new car to show off by then huh? I'd like to have one too, but I don't know if I will. If I decide that I'll have enough money for it after taking out expenses for three years of school, then I'll buy a '68 Charger.

I guess it's time for me to "cut out" now, so I'll close

and be waiting for your next
letter. So long now...

With Love,
"Ellsworth"

P.S. Nancy, thanks a lot for that
medal. Sure is a nice one.
Also, I already have a
Bible.

$$11 \div x = 12 - x \quad \text{MAY } 5$$

Dear All,
$$\frac{11}{x} = 12 - x ,$$
$$\frac{11}{1} = 12 \mp x$$

Sorry for not writing for so long, but I haven't felt like doing anything at all lately. You'll be glad to hear that I'm not "out there in the jungles fighting" at the present. But the reason why, is that same reason why I haven't written for awhile. Yes, I'm in the hospital again, this time with Malaria. The mosquito finally got me. I have the "Fallociprium" type which, previous to the recent discovery of its cure, was killing many soldiers over here. I first contracted the disease near the last of April and the Doctor says that I'll be out 'til June.

2

Boy, there have been a few sick days so far. For a while there, my temperature was frequently above 105° and I was quite miserable. I feel pretty good now – just a back-ache and weakness. But the Doctor says I will probably have one more (less severe) fever attack. After that, things should be okay if I keep on taking my pills.

I got sent to the hospital during a pretty "hot" time for my battalion. We have been up North of Hué on a big operation in "A Shau" Valley. We went up there about two weeks ago, and it didn't take long to learn that there were many gooks there.

3

Only a few days had gone by when when we first ran into booby-traps. We lost two "point-men" (usually the victim) to explosive-type booby-traps. The first one got his leg ripped up, and the next one got it in the back of the head (through his steel helmet.) Then I took over as point-man. I just kept my eyes open for anything suspicious and found the booby traps before they found me. I'm pretty lucky because I made it through that okay, and by the time I get back with my company, they will have moved back down by Da Nang. Also, I think the worst part of the war, will

4

also be over by then. Meanwhile, I'll just sit in bed and read in the news that ("A Shau Valley" is going to be the "hottest" place in Nam soon. — My Opinion —) Really, it sure has the potential. "Charlie" is so well-armed and fortified up there, that it is scary.

A bit of good news — I was recommended to be promoted to Specialist/4 (equivilent to corporal) by the company's most decorated man and my platoon leader. I may get my promotion orders while I'm still in the hospital, I hope so. Also I was made "team-leader" – an E-5 sergeant's position. I don't have enough time-in to make that grade tho.

5

Usually, the earliest anyone makes sergeant over here, is after about 9 or 10 months. —that is, providing he's only a Pfc to start with. Anyhow, it will mean more money to me over here — about $40 per month.

Speaking of money, I will be at this hospital for about a month, and all I've got left is $3.50 With a snack-bar here etc., I could use a few more dollars. About $15.00 would be about right. So if you could rush it as fast as possible, I'll make it.

You know, this hospital-ization may have been for the better. On the day that I got sick, my com—

6   MAY 6

pany left on a "combat assault" clear up to the D.M.Z. I haven't heard anything about what's going on up there since, though! I hope they're making out okay as things may well be rough there. Actually, we were only 7 miles from the DMZ to start with. May 9th is supposed to mark the end of our mission up North so my company only has 3 more days to sweat.

I imagine that my mail will take a long time to find me at first. Usually, hospitalization really screws a guys mail up over here! Guess I'll just have to sit and wait for it patiently. At least

7

I am able to watch tele-
vision and listen to the
radio and do lots of reading.
Also, in 7 days, my spleen
will have mostly healed
and I can walk around
and go to the movies, P.X. etc.
By my calculations, it's
only three more weeks 'til
fishing season opens there.
Start cleaning up the
fishing gear, Bill, and
get ready to go getem'.
Wish I was there for it
too, but I'll make it next
year.
Have you got your
driver's liscence Bill?
Just a few more weeks
and you'll be old enough
to buy cigarettes!
And Jim, have you sold
your bomb yet? Last I

8

heard, you had a possible buyer on the hook. How much were you asking for it? Did you ever fix it up anymore? I suppose my old beast is still chuggin' along, huh?

And how is my Mother, Father & Grandma doing? Still creaking by, huh. One Montana Spring should be enough to stand you all up. There's nothing like a warm Montana May day.

I just got word that I can call you all, tomorrow morning. What a surprise! It will be evening there and I hope not too late. I just know that you'll all forget to say "Over" when you're done talking. I've got to

9

call collect but I instist
that you pay for it out of
the money I'm sending home.
I know it will be a
worth-while investment
of a few dollars for me.
I will have tried to
not say to much of what
I'm saying in this letter.
I'll probably blab most of
it though.
Well, I guess I'll close
now and try to say
what I've missed, when
I call tomorrow. I
hope everyone is still
feeling alright. You
all take care now.

Love,
Your Son,
Bob

①   June 19

Dear Eve & George,

    Hi, how's the world? I just remembered that you said you were going back to "G.F." around the 14th. So now I'm debating whether to send this to *your* home or to send it to the folks.' I wish you would have told me how long you intended to stay there. I guess I'll send it to Oregon so you'll have it when you return.

    Well, you probably read my last letter to G.F., so just about anything I could say would be old news to you. But I'll try to say something new.

    My outfit is still high upon this mountain where we've been building bunkers for the last 10 days or so. Everything is routine as hell up here so I

—OVER—

②hope we leave here before I lose my mind. Intelligence sources say that a battalion of N.V.A. soldiers is headed this way so, unless we leave pretty soon, we may see a little action yet.

How was your trip back to Montana? I hope it was an enjoyable one. I know it most likely was for the kids. I'll bet I won't even be able to recognize the kids when I get back as they will be about $1\frac{1}{2}$ years older than they were last time I saw them. Wish I had a picture of them now. I sure look forward to an enjoyable visit with you all when I get back.

Please excuse this atrocious looking paper, but I had gotten this far along before the paper got dirty. The marks, incidently, are the imprints of a jungle combat boot.

June 23

I sent a package home a few days ago. You may still have

③

been at the Jewell household when (if) it arrived. It contained a very crude chalice, a small metal cruit, and a glass kerosene lamp. All of them, I think, are unique, and maybe even antique, souvineers of Nam. The chalice could be silver but is probably just lead. The cruit is small but a finely made item. I found it, and the chalice, in an old bombed ruin of a Church deep in the boondocks of Viet Nam. I had doubts about my being allowed to keep them, so I checked with the chaplain and he said it was okay. The little glass lamp, I found on a small shrine table of a Viet Cong gook. It also was rather crude, but had the "uniqueness" appeal to it.

— OVER —

④ I hope they all made it home in one piece.

I had a heck of a time getting any sleep last night. A swarm of rats moved into our bunker with us and really caused a commotion. We had almost fallen asleep when they started tearing around the bunker, jumping on us, and squealing like little pigs. Well, I'll tell ya— that turned our peaceful little bunker into W.W. III. I have "a thing" about rats in the first place, so I really put my heart into the battle! We had a flashlight with which we were able to guide our blows at first, but during one exciting moment, a buddy broke it over one of the rats. And then it was too dark to see where we were striking so the rats chased us out thus ending the war. We spent the rest of the night, freezing,

(5)

on top of our own bunker while
the rats ransacked below us.
Damn rats!

Today, my fire-team and myself
are on top of another mountain,
away from our company. We
were sent over here to set up
a lookout post. It's nice to
be away from all the work-details.
Lots of time to ourselves and
we are still reasonably safe
from the "dinks", as we have
air-evacuation priority in case
of trouble. We're up 3,000
feet above the valley below.
Quite a beautiful view! We
can see Da Nang — thirty miles
to the N.E., Chu Lai — forty miles
to the S.E., the ocean — fifty miles
to the East, and hundreds of miles
of mountains behind us to the West.
We can see clear into Thailand
from here. I've borrowed a friend's

(6)

camera so I think I'll get some photos from up here. I owe a few people some pictures so I'd _better_ start taking some. I'll be sure to get some to you too. Okay?

Well, that's about it for now. I hope you got a chance to read my last letter home too, during your visit there. Hope everyone is happy after the visit to Montana. I'll be seeing you.

With Love, Bob
Sp/4

My new rank, remember?